S0-EIG-178

Internet!
I Didn't Know You Could Do That...™

Alan R. Neibauer

SYBEX®

San Francisco • Paris • Düsseldorf • Soest • London

Associate Publishers: Amy Romanoff, Cheryl Applewood
Contracts and Licensing Manager: Kristine O'Callaghan
Acquisitions & Developmental Editor: Sherry Bonelli
Editor: Rebecca Rider
Technical Editor: Kevin O'Brien
Book Designers: Franz Baumhackl, Kate Kaminski
Electronic Publishing Specialist: Franz Baumhackl
Project Team Leader: Teresa Trego
Proofreader: Jennifer Campbell
Indexer: Nancy Guenther
Companion CD: Ginger Warner
Cover Designer: Daniel Ziegler
Cover and Chapter Photographs: PhotoDisc

To Barbara

Acknowledgments

No book is really ever the effort of only one person. It took a number of people to complete this book, and I am forever grateful to all of them.

My thanks to AOL expert Laura Arendal for pitching in at the last moment and doing such a wonderful job with the AOL section of this book. Laura is the author of her own book devoted to AOL, and she was kind enough to add her expertise to this project.

My appreciation to everyone at Sybex who helped with this book, especially Acquisition Editor Kristine O'Callaghan, Associate Publisher Amy Romanoff, Acquisitions and Developmental Editor Sherry Bonelli, and Editor Rebecca Rider. Thanks also to Technical Editor Kevin O'Brien, Project Team Leader Teresa Trego, Electronic Publishing Specialist Franz Baumhackl, and Proofreader Jennifer Campbell.

Thanks to all of the companies, and Web site and software developers who generously granted permission to include their Web sites as illustrations in this book, and who allowed their software to appear on the accompanying CD-ROM.

I'd also want to thank all of the folks who suggested topics and Web sites: Lori Secouler, Herb Kaufman, Harvey Sweig, Kenn Venit, Miriam Greenwald, Richard Moses, Bonnie Moses, Dave Olshina, Marsha Sobel, and Curtis Philips.

Finally, my deepest appreciation and love to a remarkable woman, a Xena Warrior Princess in her own time, my wife Barbara. During the process of this book, she moved two complete households across state lines, kept the home fires burning, and the food cooking (although there were quite a few pizza nights). There is no one like her.

Table of Contents

Introduction

The Internet is one great place to be! No matter what type of information you need, what products you want to buy, or who you want to contact, you can find what you need on the Internet. I know from some very personal experiences.

Years ago, when my physician was treating me for the flu, I was able to diagnose a rash that I had as a symptom of Lyme disease. I was then able to get the treatment I needed. I found this information on an Internet health site.

More recently, my wife and I were able to save over $70,000. To make a long and agonizing story short, we needed to get public water installed in our house because the water from our well was tainted. The initial estimate from the local water company was just under $80,000. That's when my wife, Barbara, learned how to use the Internet. Through an e-mail campaign directed at government officials and agencies, water department officials and consumer groups, Barbara was able to get water installed for a very substantial savings.

So, while the Internet can be a fun place to shop and play, it can also be a very valuable resource to you and your family.

One of the best things about the Internet is that you don't even need your own computer and Internet account to take advantage of most of the topics discussed in this book and most of the free offers and resources on the Internet. You just need access to the Internet and your own e-mail account. You can get access to the Internet for free, or for very little cost. You'll find such access at local libraries and schools, Internet cafes, and other establishments that make the Internet available. If you need an e-mail account to sign up for offers and other freebies, you can get a free e-mail account, as you'll learn how to do in this book. So without your own computer and a monthly Internet charge, you can send and receive e-mail and even have your own Web page!

This book is my way of sharing some of the interesting and often unique things that you can do over the Internet. Some of the topics you'll read about in this book are not well known, others may seem familiar but you'll learn about new features and unique approaches. It may be something you've *heard* can be done over the Internet but never knew exactly *how* to do it.

How This Book Is Organized

The book is divided into parts. Each part is a collection of numbered sections that cover things to do and see on the Internet.

In *See It, Hear It, Say It,* you'll learn some entertaining things. You'll learn how you can watch television, documentaries, sporting events, and classic movies on your computer screen as you work. You'll also learn how to watch people all over the world through Web cameras, download music and make your own CD's, and chat and talk to friends, relatives, and strangers online.

Searching the Unlimited Resource is all about finding things on the Internet. Since you probably already know about using search engines like Yahoo! and Lycos, I'll show you techniques for supercharging your searches. You'll learn how to find driving directions, people, jobs, a place to live, and even a date or spouse.

In *It's About Time,* you'll learn how to keep track of your online time and keep your computer's clock on time. You'll also know what time it is at any place around the world, and you'll be able to keep track of your own time online by maintaining your schedule on the Internet.

In *News and Mail,* you'll learn to access the latest news online. You'll find out what's happening right in your own town, you'll get and manage free e-mail accounts, and you'll reduce the clutter of junk e-mail.

Free e-mail is only the tip of the freebie-iceberg on the Internet. In *More Free Stuff,* you'll learn how to get free stuff of all types, including free Internet accounts, electronic greeting cards, and your very own fax telephone number. You'll also learn how to get free software and books.

In *Enhancing the Internet Experience,* you'll learn secrets for speeding up surfing; after you are finished with this part you will be able to browse more than one site at a time and browse offline. You'll also learn how to share one phone line and one Internet account after your computers are networked.

In *Web Sites, Free or Easy,* you will learn how to grab graphics and sounds that you see online. You will also learn how to find out who owns a Web site you are interested in. You'll read about how to get your own free Web sites, how to store personal documents on the Internet, and how to register your own Web domain.

In *Buying Online,* you'll learn techniques for winning Web auctions, and finding hard-to-locate, out-of-print books and collectibles for almost any collection.

In *Getting Help*, you will find out how to get the latest device drivers for your hardware and how to upgrade Windows 98. You'll also uncover secrets for getting legal, medical, and do-it-yourself help.

The last part of this book, *Let AOL Rock Your World!,* is designed just for America Online members. Here you'll find out how to supercharge and enhance your AOL experience in ways you never thought possible. This section of the book, by the way, was written by Laura Arendal, an expert on squeezing the most out of AOL.

Each of the numbered topics in this book is organized in about the same way. After a brief introduction, you'll find two general topics—*Here's What You Need* and *Sites and Features* (in the AOL part the second section is called *Here's How It Works*).

In the *Here's What You Need* sections, you'll find out what resources you need to take advantage of the features described in the specific numbered section. In most cases, all you need is access to the Internet. In some cases, you'll need a special piece of software—which you get on the CD-Rom that comes with this book.

In *Sites and Features*, you'll learn all of the tips and techniques as well as what sites you can access on the Internet.

One word of caution. Internet sites are changing constantly. Some are just redesigned, others are taken off of the Web entirely. It is very possible that some of the Web sites described and pictured in this book may not appear the same way on your screen. Some of the sites may not even be available. We'll keep you up-to-date on as many changes as possible, and some new interesting and secret Internet facts, at the Sybex Web site, `http://www.sybex.com`.

If you have a favorite Web site that you'd like to share with other readers, drop me a note at `alan@neibauer.net`.

What Is on the CD

Many of the secrets and techniques you'll learn about in this book involve a software program, so look for this icon:

This icon means that the program described in the book is on the CD packaged with the book. The CD contains valuable programs that will enhance your Internet experience.

Some of the programs are freeware, which means you can use the program as long as you want for no charge. Other programs are shareware. You can use these programs, but are asked to pay a small fee if you like the program and you want to continue using it after the trial period has ended. In some cases, you can only use the program for a certain number of days before it expires. You'll have to register and pay for the program to continue using it.

You'll find complete information about each program when you install it, and a list of the programs in the Read.Me file on the CD.

NOTE Once again, it is important to remember that these products are being changed and updated regularly. Although we have tried to put the most recent version of the software on the CD, it is very possible that there will be a more recent version of some of this software available when you get this book. Please check the URLs that are provided for the most up-to-date information.

Downloading Software

Almost all of the programs on the CD are also available for downloading from the Internet. Downloading means that you transfer a copy of the program from the Internet to your computer. The location on the Internet where you can download the program and get more information will be listed in the text and on the readme document on the CD.

You do not need to download a copy of a program if you see the CD icon in the text. But sometimes you'll find a more recent or improved version of the program on the Web site. If you find a program that you really like and intend to use frequently, check out the Web site for the latest version.

You will also learn about programs in this book that are not included on the CD. You may want to download and try out these programs as well. Somewhere on the Web site you'll see a link for downloading the file. Its name and position varies with every program and every Web site. Usually, when you click the link, your Web browser will display a message asking if you want to open the file or save the file on your disk. Always choose the Save option. You may then see a dialog box in which you select the location to place the file and provide it with a name. There will always be a default name given, so don't change that, but you might want to make a note of the location to which the file will be saved, or you may even want to select a new location. The dialog box is much like the Save As dialog box you'll find with most Windows applications.

Unzipping Files

Files that you'll find on the CD or download are either executable programs or ZIP files.

All of the products on the CD will be executable programs with .EXE extensions. To install or run these programs, double-click the EXE file. The program will either begin running immediately or you will be guided through the steps of a setup and installation program.

Many of the files you download from the Internet, however, are ZIP files with the .ZIP extension. Because program files can be quite large, and actually require a number of individual files, they are compressed, or shrunken, and saved in a special reduced format, called a ZIP file. You can download a ZIP file in much less the time than in its uncompressed format.

To install or run a program that is in a ZIP file, you have to first unzip it. This decompresses, or expands, the files to their full actual size. In order to unzip a ZIP file, you'll need a special program called WinZip that you'll find on the CD with this book. When you click the WinZip button on the CD interface, the program (winzip70.exe) will be copied to a default location on your hard drive. Double-click the .EXE file to install it on your computer. During the installation, you will be asked if you want to use the WinZip Wizard to unzip files, or the WinZip Classic interface. Choose the option Start with WinZip Classic, and then click Next and continue with the installation process.

When you download a ZIP file from the Internet, just double-click the file's zip icon. Click I Agree in the box that appears to start WinZip and see a list of the items in the archived zip file. Click the Extract button on the WinZip toolbar, choose the location where you want to place the files in the box that appears, and then click Extract.

Internet Tool Pack

In addition to WinZip, which you'll need to unzip some programs, you'll also find three other programs on the CD for general Internet surfing:

Neoplanet   Is a complete Web browser, like Microsoft Internet Explorer and Netscape Navigator. If you do not have a Web browser, or want to try a fresh new approach to browsing, Install Neoplanet from the CD.

LockDown 2000 Is a program that provides some security against unauthorized access to your computer while you are on the Internet.

ClipCache Lets you copy multiple items into the Windows clipboard, which you'll find useful for copying Web site addresses, graphics, or other items of interest on the Internet.

An Internet Potpourri

There are an unfathomable number of places to go on the Internet for help of all kinds. We'll touched on some of them in this book, but you will certainly find thousands of additional sites on your own, and you will also get recommendations from friends and relatives. You'll see Internet sites in company advertisements, and hear them in television and radio announcements. You can find, buy, and sell just about everything.

In addition to the sites in this book, here are a few that have been recommended to me by interested observers:

◆ For online gambling, try http://www.gamingclub.com or `http://www.gambling.com`.

◆ For earthquake information try `http://gldss7.cr.usgs.gov`.

◆ To track airlines in flight go to `http://www.thetrip.com/usertools/flighttracking`.

◆ To find out the time of high and low tides visit `http://www.nws.mbay.net`

◆ To buy cars go to `http://www.autobytel.com`, `http://www.carpoint.msn.com`, `http://www.autovantage.com`, `http://www.autoweb.com`, or `http://www.kbb.com`.

◆ Finally, when you want to make some hopefully very long range plans, the last Web site you may want to visit is `http://www.funeralsoftware.com`.

See It, Hear It, Say It

Through the Internet, you can get sights and sounds from around the world. You can listen to music, watch television and video, and create your own personal collection of music to play at your convenience. You can even watch real people do real things via video cameras placed at interesting locations. You can view these videos from your computer through the Web 24 hours a day. You can also enjoy chatting with friends and strangers over the Internet; you can even talk in real-time—just as if you were on the telephone.

1 Mix Learning with Pleasure

This is something you'll really love—it's one of my favorites. If you feel guilty about it, just tell people it's educational and beneficial, similar to the way playing games improves hand-eye coordination. It actually is educational. But the real reason you'll like this one is because it is just so much fun.

Watch Live News, TV, and the Classics of Hollywood

You can watch old movies and live television right on your computer screen. You can view documentaries and news (that's the educational part), watch sports programs, and listen to music and live on-air radio. Beats the heck out of watching the Windows screen saver when you're bored at work.

Here's What You Need

The quality of a movie or TV broadcast image on your screen depends on your screen resolution, the number of colors, and the speed of your Internet connection. As a general rule of thumb, the higher the resolution and the faster the connection the better the image. You can change your screen resolution using the Display applet in the Windows Control Panel. You'll also need a working sound card.

Windows Media Player and Real Player

Next, you'll need to have both Windows Media Player and a program called Real Player installed on your system. That's no problem because both are free (Real Player is on the CD with this book, making acquiring it even easier!). No special hardware is required. Why both programs? When you run a music or video file on the Internet, it automatically accesses one of these programs (most Web sites that display video files contain links to download Windows Media Player or Real Player). You might have your choice of which to use, but often the Web site just tries to run one of them automatically. Having both programs installed means you'll be able to view and hear almost anything.

If you do not have the necessary program installed when you try to view a multimedia file, you'll be asked if you want to download the file to your computer anyway. If you get this message, just say No—the file won't do you much good without the program installed, and video files can be extremely large and time-consuming to download. Make a note of the site you visited for the file, then install both Windows Media Player and Real Player (you'll learn how to do this later in this section) and then try again.

Both Real Player and Windows Media Player use a "streaming" sort of routine. This means that you don't have to wait until the entire movie or sound file is downloaded to your computer to view or listen to it. The show begins as soon as a portion of the file is downloaded, and then continues playing as more comes in. If Internet traffic is busy, however, you may notice some delay between pieces of the file transmission.

To see if you have Windows Media Player, follow these steps:

1. Try Start ➣ Programs ➣ Accessories ➣ Entertainment ➣ Windows Media Player.

2. If that is not an option, try Start ➣ Find ➣ Files or Folders.

3. Type MPLAYER and click Find Now.

4. Double-click MPLAYER2 if it is listed in the window.

Compare the program on your screen with the one shown in Figure 1.1.

If the program does appear, select Help ➣ Check for Player Upgrade. Windows dials into your Internet Service Provider (ISP), connects to the appropriate site, and sees if you have the most recent version. Just follow the instructions on screen if you need to download a newer release.

FIGURE 1.1 Windows Media Player

If the program is not already installed, or it does not appear anything like the one shown here, navigate to `http://www.microsoft.com/windows/mediaplayer/default.asp` and download it for free. To see if you have Real Player installed and ready, follow these steps:

1. Start ➢ Programs ➢ Real ➢ Real Player G2.

2. If that is not an option, click Start ➢ Find ➢ Files or Folders.

3. Type **REALPLAY** and click Find Now.

4. Double-click Real Player if it is listed in the window.

Compare it to the one shown in Figure 1.2.

FIGURE 1.2 Real Player

If the program does appear, click Help ➤ Check for Upgrade to dial into your ISP, connect to the appropriate site and see if you have the most recent version. Just follow the instructions on screen if you need to download a newer release.

If the program is not already installed, or it does not appear anything like the one shown here, you'll find a trial version of it on the CD with this book. You can also purchase the complete version, called RealPlayer Plus, at `http://www.real.com`.

While there are important differences between the free and paid versions of the program, start out with the free one to make sure you like it.

QuickTime

While you're downloading software, it might also help to have Apple Computer, Inc.'s QuickTime player installed on your system. There are some video files that are designed solely for that format, and they cannot be viewed on the other players. The QuickTime viewer is also free for downloading from `http://www.apple.com/quicktime`. To download the player, you'll need to enter your e-mail address and select a format—either for the Macintosh or Windows.

What you actually download is an installation program that is about 700KB. You then run that program to reconnect to the Internet in order to download the QuickTime viewer itself. You can choose from three flavors of the viewer—Minimum, Full, and Custom. It is best to choose Full to be able to play the widest variety of movies.

Sites and Features

Once you are armed with both Real Player and Windows Media Player, you can use them to access interesting video sites, or go to some directly yourself. The following descriptions cover some of these sites in more detail.

Howdy Partner

To get to old westerns navigate to http://wwww.westerns.com/frame.htm and click the first screen. From this page, you can either choose to watch the week's featured movie, or click any of the links on the left.

Clicking Theater displays a catalog of films that are available. When you select the film you want to watch, you'll see details about it as shown in Figure 1.3. Click the graphic of the film to start viewing it. Windows Media Player will begin, and the movie will download for viewing.

FIGURE 1.3   Click the graphic to run the film.

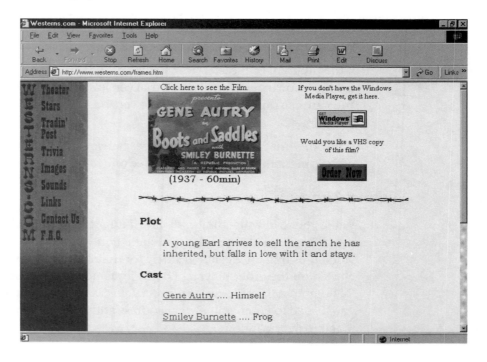

What's great about Westerns.com is the number of films available. Some of the films are even available on old-fashioned videocassette; you can order these online from Westerns.com.

Live TV

AmericaOne.com is a family-oriented television network. This site provides all of its programming live on the Internet as well. Some of their programming consist of old films and television shows, and those wonderful action serials that brought us old-folks into the Saturday matinee each week. The content is reminiscent of the material available on Westerns.com, but AmericaOne.com also offers plenty of children's programming and many educational shows as well. For a program schedule, navigate to `http://www.americaone.com` and click Schedule.

When you get to AmericaOne.com, click the animated graphic that says Click Here Watch Us On The Web. To start viewing the television broadcast, click the large television screen in the Web site. Whatever channel is broadcasting currently will appear in a Windows Media Player window.

N O T E If you like television theme songs, you can listen to hundreds of them, old and new, and see scenes from the shows at `http://stl.interspeed.net/TvJukebox`.

Take Your Choice

To access all sorts of films, television shows, and radio—both live and on demand—navigate to Broadcast.com. This site offers the widest variety of broadcasts in several areas. Usually, one special item is featured. You can also scan through items in a variety of categories.

By selecting Video (one of the categories), you can access the site's Video on Demand area. You'll need to register with Broadcast.com to access the videos, but registration is free. Here you can choose from its archive of video files.

Using the Software

When you run sound or video files from the Internet, the appropriate program will be started automatically (as long as you have it installed). You can also start either Windows Media Player or Real Player from the Start ➤ Programs menu on the desktop to access a wide range of files and features.

Windows Media Player   Start Windows Media Player from the desktop using Programs ➤ Acces-sories ➤ Entertainment ➤ Windows Media Player. Take a look at some of the highlights of the Windows Media Player.

The Favorites Menu   Offers you the option of choosing from a number of preset channels—it lists many Web sites where you can find sound and video files. You can also click Web Events to access the Microsoft Web events site: `http://windowsmedia.microsoft.com`. This is a great site to go to for a wide variety of video and music files. Choose from a list of audio and video headlines or from these categories:

The File Menu   Lets you open files on your disk.

The View Menu   Lets you change the size of the window or display videos full screen.

The Play Menu   Lets you play, stop and move through sounds and videos.

The Go Menu   Lets you go back and forward through visited sites; it also directs you to the Web Events and Windows Media Player home pages.

The Help Menu   Gives you information about how to use Windows Media Player and how to check for program upgrades.

The controls for playing files are shown here:

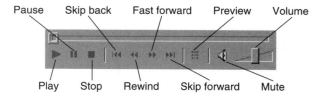

Real Player   Real Player comes in several versions, so you should make sure you have the most recent, as explained earlier. Start Real Player using Start ➤ Programs ➤ Real ➤ Real Player G2 or by selecting any Real Player file on the Internet. Some of the most useful portions of this program are described below.

The Preset Menu   Works like Internet Explorer Favorites, except that it already has preset categories that let you access popular sites.

The Sites Menu   Lets you access Web sites from which you can choose music or video files.

The Control Panel   Lists preset channels. You can use it as an alternative to the menus at the top of the Real Player screen or you can search for files based on keywords. The Control Panel is located along the left of the window. Click the channel you want to play, or scroll using the up and down arrows:

The Text Box Search Search for files by entering a keyword in the text box at the bottom of the window, then click Search.

EarthTuner One of my favorite ways to access live audio and video broadcasts is a program called EarthTuner that contains a database of over 1,400 stations from around the world. You'll find a 15-day trial of this program on the CD that comes with this book, or you can download it from `http://www` `.digiband.com`.

This is one great program. When you first start the program, it gives you the opportunity to connect to the Digiband Web site to download the latest database of stations, and to make EarthTuner the default player for audio and video. I'd suggest choosing No here to keep on using Windows Media Player or Real Player as your default player. This way, if you choose to delete the trial version from your system, you won't have any problems viewing multimedia files.

You can search for a station by its location or format, but it is more fun to select countries from the animated globe. Just drag the globe to rotate it, and click the country for the broadcast you want to hear.

As shown in Figure 1.4, pointing or clicking on the globe shows you not only the location, but the number of station Web sites, audio broadcasts, and video broadcasts in the database. Double-click the location, or click the Browse tab to see a detailed list of locations and stations. Double-click a link to start the broadcast or to connect to the Web site.

By holding down the right mouse button and drawing a box, you can also zoom in on the globe for a closer look.

All of the standard controls for playing, pausing, forwarding and rewinding are provided, and you can even create a list of preset channels for quick access to your favorites.

FIGURE 1.4 Tuning the globe in EarthTuner

Internet Explorer Radio Toolbar If you have Internet Explorer 5, you can also select and listen to live radio broadcasts using the Radio Toolbar:

If the bar is not already displayed when you start Internet Explorer, right-click the toolbar already shown, and select Radio from the menu that appears.

To use this feature and select a radio station, click Radio Stations in the toolbar and choose Radio Station Guide from the menu. The browser will access a Web site from which you can choose a station to listen to. Stations you select will later be listed in the Radio Stations menu for your convenience.

Imagine the Opportunities

I've listed just a few of the sites here where you can access audio and video files—there are plenty of others.

At `http://www.spinner.com`, for example, you can download the free Spinner-Plus software. When you run the program, it connects to the Spinner Web site and lets you select a channel of music to listen to. Here are some other sites where you can access music, video, and live television:

- ◆ `http://www.cdnow.com`
- ◆ `http://www.film.com`
- ◆ `http://www.musicnet.com`
- ◆ `http://www.hollywoodandvine.com`

2 Discover Real Time

Do you want to feel like a secret agent spying on the enemy, or are you just curious about what's going on in other parts of the world? You can watch real people doing real things, and view some of nature's bounty, live on the Web.

View Real Life around the World

Web cameras (AKA Webcams) are cameras placed at various locations around the world that broadcast their images on the Internet. Most of the cameras are on 24/7—24 hours a day, seven days a week—so you can always find something to watch.

Here's What You Need

You'll need access to the Internet. You should also have the Real Player and Microsoft Media Player programs installed if you want to see live video rather than still pictures.

Sites and Features

You may not find all Webcams very interesting to look at. Depending on the visibility provided by the weather, or the time of day, you could be looking at a deserted street in Paris or the clouds hanging over Mount Fuji. But most of the cams are worth looking at periodically just for curiosity's sake. Some may be aimed at locations you are familiar with or plan to visit. Others may be broadcasting a beautiful natural scene or just the world of plain folks as they pass by the camera lens. There's one site, for example, `http://www.electrolux.com/node230.asp`, filmed from the inside of a refrigerator. From this site, you can see what the fruits and vegetables see when the door closes, and what we non-edibles look like when the door opens. This finally answers the question "Does the light really go off when you close the door?"

NOTE The vast majority of the Web cameras are free, but a few charge a fee. You'll have to register and give credit card information to access those sites, which are usually for adult audiences only.

There are a lot of Web cameras in people's homes, offices, and dorm rooms. Tune in to see what these folks are doing, or not doing, at any time. The cameras are all over the world so don't be surprised if you can peek at life in Peking, admire a scene from Amsterdam, or just watch cats play in Katmandu. The text on the screen may be in a language you don't understand, but you can always just look at the pictures.

The majority of the cameras offer still photographs so you'll see the most recent picture taken. The pictures are updated at regular intervals, so you can click your browser's Refresh or Reload button as often as you want to see the most recent shot. Some cameras are updated every second or so, others less frequently.

Many of the sites also give you the option of watching a real video scene. If you have Windows Media Player and Real Player installed, click the link to start watching the live action in front of the camera.

You can do a search for Webcam or Web cameras, but the best place to start is at `http://www.camcity.com`. When you get to the site, click the *Go Webcams* link. This will open a page that displays the Webcam of the day. Use the options at the top of the screen to select other cameras:

Breaking News Cam   Displays a camera watching current news as it happens.

Newsletter   Lets you register for an electronic newsletter.

Webcam of the Day   Shows the day's featured site.

Search   Lets you search for a site using keywords.

Indoor   Lists sites inside buildings.

Outdoor   Lists exterior views.

Region   Lets you select a site by location.

Subject   Lets you choose a site by its subject.

Top 100   Displays the most popular Web cameras.

Some of the top 100 Webcam sites are listed in Figure 2.1. You'll see a sample screen, a rating from 1 to 5 stars, an icon representing daylight or evening view, the amount of time between updates, and a brief description. Click the sample screen to go to the site, that displays the most recently updated image.

FIGURE 2.1   Sample of CamCity's top 100 sites

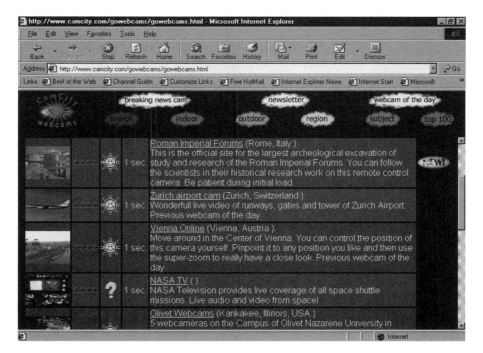

One of the most popular sites on CamCity is entitled *Here and Now—Real Life. Real Time.* You can access this site from CamCity's top 100 list, or go directly there (http://www.hereandnow.net/webcast.html).

At Here and Now, you can access several cameras with full motion video and sound in an apartment in Oberlin, Ohio. Six college friends volunteered to have their lives exposed to the world, so you can tune in any time of the day to see what's going on. You may see and hear one or more of the six watching television, sleeping on the sofa, or candidly discussing some aspect of their life.

Take your time and go through the pages of the other popular sites. You'll be able to watch a wide variety of animals at play, and be able to see what's happening at locations from Times Square in New York to oasis watering holes in Africa.

For another list of popular sites, go to `http://www.excite.com`. Once there, click Entertainment. From the Entertainment screen, click Humor and then click Web Cameras. You'll see a list that includes specific sites and Web camera directories. Along with many other sites, you can choose to see

◆ The view from the top of Mount Fuji in Japan at `http://www.sunplus.com/fuji`.

◆ The view from the top of Pike's Peak in the United States at `http://www.pikespeakcam.com`.

◆ Scenes at the Kennedy Space Center at `http://www.ambitweb.com/nasacams/nasacams.html`.

◆ What's happening at the famous Hollywood sign in California at `http://www.rfx.com/hollywood`.

You can also choose to see a list of Animal Cams featuring cows, cats, dogs, fish, rhinos, orangutans, lions, tigers, bears and other animal friends.

Another great site for Web cameras is `http://www.earthcam.com`, which groups cameras into a variety of categories. Click a category, or one of the links under a category, to see additional options.

From the EarthCam home page, you can also select one of the EarthCam Metro Sites listing major cities in the United States. Click a city link to search for a camera in that location.

Many of the Web's major search engines also give you direct links to Webcams. To access interesting sites from Yahoo, for example, go to `http://dir.yahoo.com/Computers` and then click the *Internet* link. At the new screen, click *Devices Connected to the Internet*. From this screen, you can click the *Web Cams* link to see a list of links to various sites.

Working with Webcams

Webcams can be great entertainment, and even a learning experience, but the technology that creates Webcams is still new and, in a lot of ways, experimental.

Not only do you need the proper programs installed (such as Windows Media Player and Real Player) but your computer's settings can play a major part in your Web camera enjoyment. For example, the slower your

Internet connection, the more time it takes to download and start displaying video. Real-time video might appear jumpy, with some long pauses between scenes as more information is downloaded.

You might want to try various display settings to see which one gives you the fastest and smoothest pictures. Through the Display Properties dialog box, for example, you can set the number of colors and the resolution of your screen. To open the Display Properties dialog box, right-click a blank area of the desktop, choose Properties from the shortcut menu, and click the Settings tab.

The options on Webcam sites also differ greatly. On some sites, you can choose to use either Windows Media Player or Real Player; you can also specify the speed of your connection. Even if you connect at 56K the video quality can be jumpy; try connecting again by selecting a slow connection speed from the Webcam site.

Keep in mind that Webcam video takes up a lot of resources, both on the Internet and on your computer. If you can't seem to get acceptable performance, try reconnecting at a later time when the Webcam site, and your ISP, might be less busy.

3 Dance to the Music, for Free!

Free music and complete CDs are available on the Internet. Listen to music while you work, or download it for easy listening at any other time.

Download and Listen to Music—Create Your Own CDs

If you have a CD recorder, you can even make your own custom CD with all of your favorite tracks! If you don't have a CD recorder, you can save music for playback on your hard disk, zip disk, or other high-speed storage device.

Here's What You Need

Until recently, sound and music files were transmitted through the Internet in a variety of formats (such as WAV and MIDI). Full-length music files could be quite large, however, and often never had the clarity of the original sounds.

A new music format has been developed that changes all that. With Moving Pictures Experts Group (MPEG) Audio Level 3 (known as MP3), music can be compressed by a factor of 12 and still retain its CD quality. In theory, using MP3, a complete CD can be downloaded over the Internet in about five minutes. In practice, with a 56K modem, you can get about one minute of music or several minutes of an audio book in three to five minutes. You can then play the music from your computer's hard drive or transfer it to a handheld device that you can take with you.

If you have a CD recorder, you can download or copy music tracks to your computer, and then make your own CD. The process takes a few steps, but it's worth it to be the life of the party.

N O T E   Diamond Multimedia markets the Rio, a portable device that connects to your computer's printer port to download and play music that you've received over the Internet. For more information, go to `http://www.diamondmm.com`.

In addition to your Internet connection, you'll need a program that plays music in the MP3 format. The most recent versions of Windows Media Player and Real Player play MP3 files, so you can use the version of Real Player on the CD with this book. You'll also find the program MP3 CD Maker on the CD; this program plays MP3 music and lets you record MP3 files on your recordable CD.

You might have heard or read stories about illegal downloading of music with MP3. Actually, MP3 is just a music format. You may use it legally to listen to music if the song's owner has given permission for it to be downloaded and played. Sites such as `http://www.mp3.com` only provide legal music for downloading and listening. However, a new format has come along recently to help protect the rights of musical artists. The format, known as Liquid Audio, adds a special code to music so only the person who purchases it can play it.

Let's look at how you can get free music and then we will look at some other programs for playing it.

Sites and Features

There are a growing number of sites where you can find MP3 files. However, the majority of MP3 music on the Internet is not free. Music is protected by copyright, and the music industry is using MP3 as a way to sell music. You can purchase individual tracks or complete CDs, download it, and then play it at your convenience. You can also purchase CDs and have them delivered to your home. Still, there are thousands of MP3 files that are free, especially from newer recording artists who are trying to get exposure.

There are about a zillion places to find MP3 music and information, including the following sites:

◆ `http://www.mp3.com`

◆ `http://www.mp3now.com`

◆ `http://www.mp3site.com`

◆ `http://crossbones.freeservers.com/mp3page.htm`

Let's take a look at two of the sites in a little more detail.

MP3.COM

To download MP3 software and music, and to learn all about MP3, navigate to `http://www.mp3.com`, a site that offers hundreds of free music files in a wide variety of categories. On this home page, there are links that take you to informative pages about MP3 music, as well as links to browse for free music by genre. The site also contains links to top songs, featured artists, MP3 software and hardware, and top news stories from the music industry.

When you choose a genre of music, you'll see a page similar to the one in Figure 3.1. You can then select a sub-category, choose a featured song, scan the top 40, or choose one of the newly added songs.

FIGURE 3.1 Selecting MP3 tracks

Click Play to listen to the featured song, or click Save to download the song to your computer. Once the file is downloaded, it will be played automatically if you have Windows Media Player or another MP3 player program installed.

To listen to one of the other titles on the page, click the Instant Play link next to its name. Click the title link to see details such as those shown here:

MP3now.com

If you're looking for MP3 music links and information, navigate to http://www.mp3now.com. The options on the site's home page, shown in Figure 3.2, give you access to a variety of music sources, software, hardware, and news.

FIGURE 3.2   MP3now.com

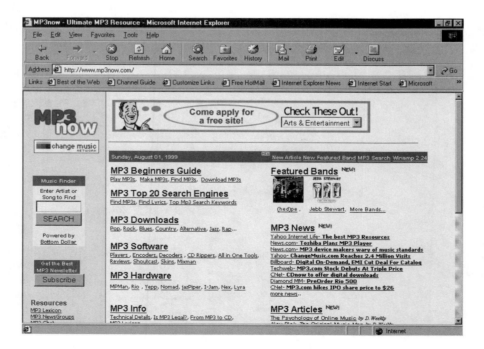

Much of the music you find through MP3now.com is not free, but can be purchased and downloaded, or order to be delivered to your door. By clicking the link Free Music under the heading MP3 Top 100 Charts, however, you can access a list of music for free downloading.

Just click the title you're interested in to download and play. At the bottom of the list you'll find a handy search feature to locate additional titles:

Your Own Jukebox

In addition to Windows Media Player and Real Player, there are lots of programs for playing MP3 music. Much of it is distributed as shareware, which you can download over the Internet. The programs not only play MP3 and other music files, but they let you create your own jukebox with music stored on your hard disk played in any order. Just be aware that music files can be quite large and take up a lot of hard disk space.

The most popular of these programs is WINAMP, a shareware program that supports most of the common audio file formats, including MP3, WAV, MOD, XM, IT, S3M, VOC, CDDA, WMA, and MIDI. You can download WINAMP from `http://ww.winamp.com`.

NOTE See "Making Your Own CDs" later in this section to learn how to use MP3 CD Maker to play MP3 files on your computer.

When you first install WINAMP, you'll see the options shown in Figure 3.3. You can select to automatically play audio CDs that you insert in your CD-ROM drive and where WINAMP icons are placed. You can also select to make WINAMP the default player for all music and audio files, rather than Windows Media Player. If you make it the default player, it will begin when you choose to play a MP3 file from the Internet or when you double-click an MP3 file in Windows.

FIGURE 3.3 Setting up WINAMP

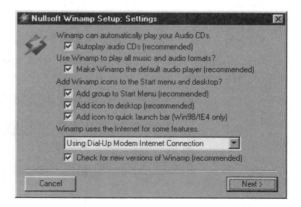

The WINAMP console is shown in Figure 3.4. It consists of the Main Window, Equalizer, Playlist Editor, and Mini Browser.

FIGURE 3.4 Running WINAMP

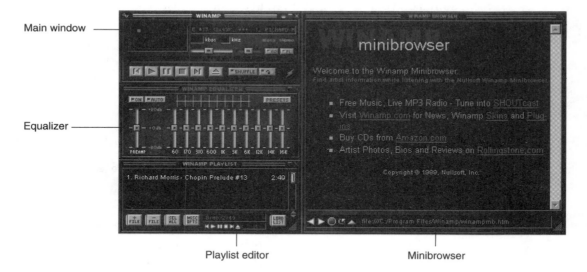

Main window

Equalizer

Playlist editor

Minibrowser

Use the buttons in the Main Window to play, stop, pause, and fast forward and reverse the current title. Right-click a button to see its function and an alternate keystroke combination.

Most of the buttons perform more than one function, depending on how you click them, as shown in Table 3.1. Above the buttons are controls for the volume and balance, and for the Equalizer and Playlist Editor. Information about the item on the top of the list, or the one playing, appears under the WINAMP title bar.

TABLE 3.1   Functions of WINAMP Buttons

Button	Click	Ctrl+Click	Shift+Click
Previous	Previous	Start of list	Rewind
Play	Play	Open Location	Open File
Pause	Pause		
Stop	Stop		Fadeout
Next	Next	End Of List	Fast Forward
Open	Open File	Open Location	Open Directory

The WINAMP Equalizer has sliders for controlling the range of the music; Playlist lists the titles to be played. Items on the Playlist play in order, one after the other. To add additional songs to the Playlist, you can drag the file's icon to the Playlist window, or click the + File button to choose the file from the Open dialog box. Use the –File button to delete a file.

To control other aspects of WINAMP, right-click the Main Window, Equalizer, or Playlist to display the shortcut menu.

You can choose which parts of the console to display, click Playback to control how files are played and click Visualization to fine-tune how the Equalizer and other elements appear. Use the Options menu to change other aspects.

Use the Mini Browser to access MP3 sources from within WINAMP. By clicking a link in the mini browser, you can connect to the Internet and see the Internet page in the Mini Browser window displayed.

One interesting and fun aspect of WINAMP is the ability to change its appearance using skins. A *skin* is a special file that you can download from the Internet to personalize the console's appearance. Figure 3.6 shows how WINAMP looks with an alternative skin.

FIGURE 3.5   Alternate WINAMP skin

Here's how to use skins.

1. Download a skin from the Internet. There are plenty of places to find skins, including the sites listed here:

◆ http://www.customize.org (this site contains skins for other products as well, not just Winamp skins.)

◆ http://www.1001winampskins.com

◆ http://www.infonet.ee/arthemes/winamp/skins.htm

◆ http://startrek.fns.net.fsn.net/download/skins.html

◆ http://www.winamp-skins.com

2. Place the skin in the Program Files/WinAmp/Skins folder. If a skin is downloaded as a zip file, do not unzip it, just move the entire file to the folder.

3. Start WINAMP.

4. Press ALT+S to open the Skin Browser window.

5. Click the skin to use. From the Skin Browser window, you can also choose to download skins from the Internet, or change the folder where your skins are located.

6. Click Close.

Of course, WINAMP isn't the only program you can use to create your own jukebox. Here are two popular programs available for downloading: Real-Jukebox at `http://www.real.com/products/realjukebox/index.html` and MusicMatch jukebox at `http://www.musicmatch.com`.

Making Your Own CDs

If you have a CD recorder, you can make your own CDs from your favorite tracks. The trick, and it really isn't complicated, is to put your MP3 music into the industry-standard WAV format. This process is called *decoding*, which is the opposite of encoding (converting a WAV file to MP3 format).

If you downloaded an MP3 file from the Internet, you can convert the file into WAV by using a type of program called a *decoder*. The decoder reads the MP3 data and creates a WAV file. You can then save the WAV file to your CD using the recording software that came with the CD recorder. For a list of decoders that you can download, go to MP3.COM's page at `http://mp3 .com/software/windows/encodersrest.html`.

Your own CDs aren't limited to MP3 files that you download. You can also take tracks off of your favorite audio CDs and save them on your own CD or to your hard drive. This is the job of a *ripper*. A ripper is a program that extracts an audio CD track into your computer as a high-quality WAV file on your hard disk. You then burn the WAV file to your recordable CD.

For a list of rippers that you can download, go to MP3.com's page at `http:// mp3.com/software/windows/cdrippersrest.html`.

As an example of making your own CDs, we'll look at the program MP3 CD Maker from ZY2000. You'll find a demonstration copy of the program on the CD with this book, or you can download it from `http://www.zy2000.com`. The demo version lets you record just four MP3 tracks, but you can use it to play an unlimited number.

MP3 CD Maker, shown in Figure 3.6, automatically records MP3 files onto your CD, handling the decoding as it records. The program supports most of the popular CD recording hardware.

FIGURE 3.6 Using MP3 CD Maker

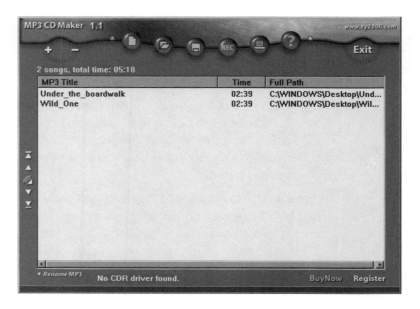

To make a CD with MP3 CD Maker, you have to create a project list of MP3 files. To create a project list, click the Add MP3 button, then click the plus sign in the upper-left corner of the window. This will access the Open dialog box in which you can select the files you want to record. The files will then be listed in the MP3 CD Maker window. You can use the buttons along the left of the window to change the order in which they will be recorded on your CD, or, after selecting a title in the main window, you can click the Play button, as shown here:

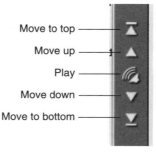

You use the buttons along the top of the window to work with the project:

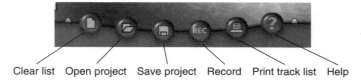

To save the project list for recording later, click Save Project, enter a project name in the box that appears, and click Save. Project files are stored with the MPJ extension. When you are ready to record the CD, click the Open Project button and double-click the name of the project.

When the list contains the tracks you want—up to 74 minutes of music— click the Record button.

Liquid Audio

Ripping tracks from your audio CDs and recording them on your own is not really legal if you give or sell the CD to someone else. Someone who should get a royalty each time the track is sold owns the music on the tracks. That's the reason there's some controversy over the MP3 format.

To allow easy purchasing and downloading of music over the Internet, however, a new format has been developed called Liquid Audio. Liquid Audio has all of the convenience of MP3 but it protects the music's owners.

Each Liquid Audio file contains a digital imprint called the Genuine Music Mark that displays the artist's name and copyright information. Liquid Audio tracks cannot be played unless they contain the imprint. If you copy the track to another disk or to a writeable CD, the music is copied but not the imprint, so you can't play the song on any machine except the one you used to download it.

You can download a free Liquid Audio player, music tracks, and other Liquid Audio programs from: http://www.liquidaudio.com.

4 And You Thought E-Mail Was Fast!

Chats let you write messages back and forth to friends and strangers in real time. Unlike e-mail, which you have to send and wait until it is received, your chat buddies see your message on-screen immediately, so they can read and reply without delay. You'll get to communicate with folks you know, and you'll meet new groups of folks from around the world.

Use AOL IM Even Without Belonging!

Instant messaging and chat rooms are two great things AOL and similar services provide. But you don't need AOL to take advantage of both of these wonderful features. To learn more about AOL IM and AIM, check out *Let AOL Rock Your World!* later in this book.

Here's What You Need

All you need to chat online is access to the Internet and a free chat program. There are plenty of free programs. In this chapter, we'll look at Instant Messenger (IM) from America Online and PowWow from Tribal Voice. You'll find a copy of PowWow on the CD with the book. You'll learn how to download AOL Instant Messenger in a few minutes.

Sites and Features

Online chats all work about the same way. The folks that provide your chat software have a big computer somewhere out there. When you want to chat with someone, you start the chat program, which connects to that big computer to see a list of other people that are connected at the same time you are. You choose who you want to chat with and start sending messages.

All of your communications are channeled through the company's computer, so it's like having instant e-mail. In addition, with PowWow, you can have a private chat with someone. You can speak and listen using your microphone and speakers just as if you were talking on the telephone.

Because of the vast number of folks who belong to AOL, however, let's start by looking at their IM program.

AOL Instant Messenger

America Online is famous for its Instant Messenger (IM) feature. If you're an AOL member and online, you can tell when a pal who also has AOL is online. You can then send them an instant message to say "Hi. Let's talk." Your message pops up on their screen, so you can start having a private conversation by writing back and forth.

You can get the benefits of AOL IM even if you're not an AOL member. You can send and receive instant messages from your friends who are on AOL, and even friends who belong to other ISPs. The trick is to download AOL's Instant Messaging software.

To get the program, follow these steps:

1. Connect to the Internet and navigate to `http://www.aol.com`.

2. Click the *Community: AOL Instant Messenger v2.0* link or go directly to `http://www.aol.com/aim/home.html`.

3. When you see the text that says Sign Up Now, click the button labeled New Users Click Here.

4. Type a screen name from 3 to 6 characters in length, the AOL equivalent of a user name. AOL members and other Instant Messaging users will use this screen name to see if you are online.

5. Type a password.

6. Retype the password to confirm it.

7. Enter your e-mail address.

8. Click the button Continue! If the screen name you've chosen is already taken, a message will appear. Click your browser's Back or Previous button and enter another screen name. You'll have to reenter your password as well.

9. Once your screen name has been accepted, you'll see a list of platforms supported by the program, including Windows, Macintosh, and Unix.

10. Click the platform that you are using to download the software.

11. When the software has finished downloading, disconnect from the Internet.

12. Double-click the downloaded program to install it.

Now that you're registered for AOL's IM and have the program installed on your computer, you're ready to communicate.

To start the program, open the Instant Messenger icon on your desktop. Enter your screen name, if it is not already shown, and your password. Enable the Save Password box if you don't want to enter your password each time. Enable the Auto-login box if you want to connect to IM automatically when you start Instant Messenger. Click Sign On.

The program connects to your ISP, if you are not already logged on, and to the IM system. It then opens a dialog box that will show other people who are online. By default, any other IM users who know your e-mail address or screen name will be able to tell if you are online.

The first thing you should do is to create your buddy list. This is a list of IM users who you want to chat with if they are online at the same time. Adding them to your list will automatically notify you when they go online. To do this

1. Click the List Setup tab.

2. Click the Add Buddy button. The notation *New Buddy* appears in the list.

3. Type the screen name of the buddy. The screen name is the name AOL members use to identify themselves and which non-AOL members use to log onto Instant Messenger. Ask your buddies for their screen names in advance.

4. Click the Online tab.

You can communicate with buddies in two ways—instant message or chat.

An instant message is a one-to-one communication. If your buddy is online, their screen name appears in the Online tab. You'll see the total number of buddies in the list and the number of those online. To send an invitation, double-click the buddy's name or click their screen name, and then click the Immediate Message button to open the Instant Message window. Type a message and then click Send. The buddy will get a Buddy Chat Invitation message. The IM window will then open two panes: one to write your messages and the other showing the entire conversation.

If you want to communicate with more than one buddy, then open a personal chat. Here's how:

1. On the Online tab, select all of the screen names for the buddies you want in the chat room. Hold down the Ctrl key to select more than one name.

2. Click the Buddy Chat icon to open the Buddy Chat Invitation window.

3. Click Send.

You can invite a buddy to join a chat in progress. In the Chat Room window, select People on the menu bar and click Invite a Buddy to send an invitation.

Finding Buddies   If you do not know the screen name of someone you want to chat with, you can locate them using the Find feature. There are three ways to search for an online buddy—by e-mail address, screen name, and interest.

NOTE   You'll learn how to add your own name, address, and interest to the AOL database for people to search in the section *Your Buddy Profile*.

1. Select People ➤ Find a Buddy.

2. Select either By E-mail Address, By Name and Address, or By Common Interest.

3. Enter the e-mail address, name and address, or select an Interest, depending on the option you selected.

4. Click Next to find a screen name. If you select by Internet, a list of people with that interest in their profile will appear. Select a user from the list and click Finish.

When You're Occupied   If you step away from your computer, you won't be available to respond to IM or chat invitations. IM lets you have two messages, an Away and Idle message.

Use the idle message when you step away for a short time. It is automatically sent when you don't use your computer for 10 minutes. Here's how.

1. Select File ➤My Options ➤ Edit Preferences.

2. Click the Away tab.

3. Select the option labeled Auto respond with message.

4. Type the message you want to appear.

5. Click OK.

If you plan to be away from the computer, then create an Away message using these steps:

1. Select File ➤My Options ➤ Edit Preferences.

2. Click the Away tab.

3. Select the option labeled Auto respond and insert in personal profile.

4. Type the new Away message.

5. Click Add Message.

6. Click OK.

When you go away from the computer, you have to turn on the message. Select File ➤ Away Message and then choose the message you want to use. Click I'm Back when you return to your computer.

N O T E   You can block messages from certain buddies and set other options by selecting Menu ➤ Options ➤ Edit Preferences, and clicking the Controls tab.

Your Buddy Profile You can enter some information about yourself that other IM users can access, called your profile. The profile can include your name and address, as well as up to five of your hobbies or interests. Other IM users can use the profile to locate members who share an interest.

To create or edit your profile, follow these steps:

1. Connect to IM.

2. Select File ➤ My Profile.

3. Enable the check box labeled Allow People to Search for Me if you want other IM member to find you by the information in your profile.

4. Enter the profile information and click Next.

5. Enable the option labeled I am available for chat so other IM members can search for you based on interest.

6. Pull down a Choose Interest list and select a hobby or interest.

7. Click Next.

8. Enter any additional information that you want to appear on your profile.

9. Click Finish.

PowWow

When you use AOL IM, you pretty much have to know with whom you want to communicate. If you want to reach a wider audience, while still being able to have private conversations, then try PowWow from Tribal Voice.

PowWow not only has a buddy feature that shows when selected people are online, but you can jump into public conversations within groups of people called communities. You can even choose to speak privately with others in your own chat room, by writing messages or by speaking into your microphone and listening to your speakers.

You'll find a copy of PowWow on the CD with this book, or you can download it from http://www.tribalvoice.com.

When you run the program for the first time, you'll see the dialog box in Figure 4.1. Enter a screen name that you want to identify yourself with in the list of online members, enter your e-mail address as your PowWow address, and enter a password. Click Get Started to start the program and dial into your ISP if you are not already online. Once connected, you'll see the PowWow window along with the Cue Card window shown in Figure 4.2.

FIGURE 4.1 Signing on to PowWow

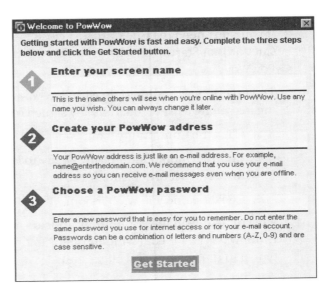

FIGURE 4.2 The PowWow and Cue Card window

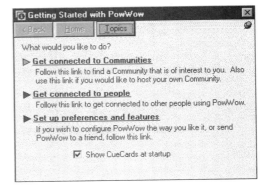

You can use the CueCards to learn how PowWow works and to select options. Just click the option that you want to select to see how to perform that task.

If you don't need the Cue Card just close the window. Disable the Show CueCards at Startup check box to skip the cards when you next start PowWow.

The first thing you should do with PowWow is join a community. This means seeing a list of folks already signed on and chatting. Here's how:

1. Click the Community icon.

2. Choose Online Community Guide to launch your Web browser and display a list of communities.

3. Click the one you want to join.

A list of people in the community appears in the PowWow list, and a window with their chat window opens to the right. To leave a message, just type it in the text box and click Send.

NOTE Click the Hear button to hear a computer-generated voice "speaking" the words that appear in the Chat window.

Rather than join the public discussion, you can invite one or more members to a private chat. Double-click the person's name in the list, or right-click and choose PowWow from the menu. A request for the PowWow is displayed on the person's screen, which they can accept or reject. If they accept the invitation, the Personal Communicator window opens. You can then write messages or click the telephone icon to talk in real time. If the person is not available to respond to your request, you'll be able to leave a message for them when they return.

PowWow is a powerful chat program that offers many sophisticated features. We've just touched on the basics of PowWow here.

Searching the Unlimited Resource

The Internet is truly amazing. How else could you get access to virtually the entire world when you're looking for something or someone? From the convenience of your home, school, local library, or Internet café, you can access the unlimited resource of people, places, and things. In this part of the book, we'll look at how to use the Internet to find things in general, and some important things in particular. Online shopping and trading will be discussed later in this book in *Buying Online*.

5 Supercharge Your Searches

By using free or inexpensive utilities, you can supercharge your searches to save time and pinpoint the information you need.

Use Multiple Search Engines at One Time

There is so much information on the Internet that sometimes it is hard to find exactly what you're looking for. Rather than use one search engine at a time, you can harness the power of multiple search companies to let them all work for you at once.

Here's What You Need

All you will need is access to the Internet and the CD that comes with this book. The CD contains a variety of programs for supercharging your searches. On the CD, you'll find these programs:

- ◆ Shetty Search
- ◆ Search By Media
- ◆ Copernic99
- ◆ MP3 Fiend
- ◆ Search Master Demo

Sites and Features

When you're looking for specific information on the Internet, where do you go? Most ISP home pages offer a search function, and you can always go directly to one of the major search sites, some of which are listed here:

- ◆ http://www.yahoo.com
- ◆ http://www.anywho.com
- ◆ http://www.excite.com
- ◆ http://www.lycos.com
- ◆ http://www.snap.com
- ◆ http://www.deja.com

If you search using one engine and still don't find what you're looking for, you have to go to another, and then another, until you find the information you want.

As an alternative to search engine hopping, you can take advantage of programs that streamline the task of searching. These programs automatically search using a number of the popular search engines at one time.

We've collected a variety of search programs for the CD that accompanies this book to illustrate the power and the versatility of software that can be downloaded from the Internet.

Shetty Search

This useful freeware program, shown in Figure 5.1, can be found on the CD, and downloaded from http://members.aol.com/satishetty.

FIGURE 5.1 **Running Shetty Search**

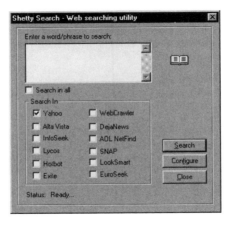

To use Shetty Search, type in the word or phrase that you're looking for, and then choose each of the search companies you'd like to use. Click the Search in All check box to use all of the companies. Then click Search.

Shetty Search dials into the Internet, if you are not already connected, and searches for your information using all of the selected sites. When the searches are complete, it opens your browser and displays the sets of results (see Figure 5.2) one after the other.

FIGURE 5.2   Results using Shetty Search

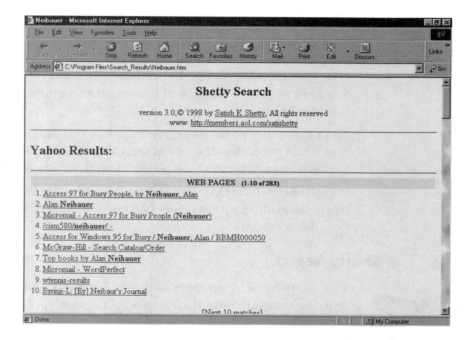

Installing Shetty Search places an icon in the system tray. Right-click the icon to open the program's window, to access a shortcut menu to search the Web, to configure the program, and to learn more about it.

Copernic99

To search the Web generally for information, or by category, try Copernic99. You'll find a copy of this program on the CD, or you can download it from http://www.copernic.com. Copernic99 not only performs a search using multiple sites, it can download pages for offline viewing and verify that links are valid.

Copernic99 opens a window (see Figure 5.3) in which you select the category to search and in which your search results will later appear. Most of the categories, and some functions such as adding new categories, are not available in the free version of the program, but if you like the program enough to buy it, Copernic99 Plus can be purchased from the manufacturer.

FIGURE 5.3   Using Copernic99

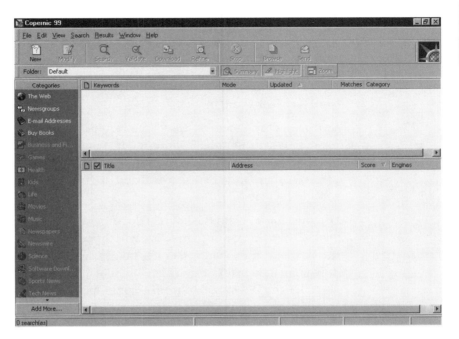

To use Copernic99, click The Web in the list of categories to open this dialog box:

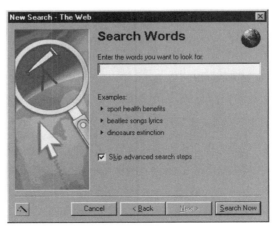

You can enter your search phase and then click Search Now, or you can turn off the check box labeled Skip Advanced Search Steps and click Next. The advanced search steps include a couple of dialog boxes for customizing how the search is performed.

When you click Search Now, Copernic99 connects to the Internet. Before performing the search, it checks with the Copernic home page for an updated list of search engines. It then searches all of the engines simultaneously, showing the search status in each.

When Copernic99 has completed its multiple search, it asks if you want to open the search results browser, which displays all of the results. Click a link to open the page in your browser window, just as you would open a site from any search engine.

If you select not to open the search results browser, you'll see your search results in the Copernic99 window. The window lists all of your searches in the upper pane, with the results of the selected search on the lower pane. If you have more than one search listed in the upper pane, click the one you want to review.

Use the check box to the left of a document title to select a document. The icons in the first column indicate whether the document is valid, invalid (no longer at the location), or has been downloaded for offline viewing. To download a page for offline viewing, select it in the Copernic99 window and click the Download button. Double-click an item to connect to the site. To open the search results browser at any time, click the Browse button in the Copernic99 toolbar or choose Results ➤ Browse.

Click the Validate button, or choose Results ➤ Validate to check all or selected documents to make sure they are still available. Click the Download button, or choose Results ➤ Download, to download all or selected documents for offline viewing.

You can also save the search results on your disk for later viewing or for use with another program. Choose File ➤ Export to open the Export Search dialog box.

Enter a name for the file, then pull down the Save As Type list, choose the format you want to save the file in, and click Save. Copernic99 saves your search results when you exit the program. The next time you start Copernic, your previous searches will still be listed. You can still access any of the documents or refine the search as desired. To delete a search from the window, right-click it and select Delete from the shortcut menu.

Search Master

Another popular search program is Search Master. You'll find a demonstration version of the program on the CD, or you can download it from http://www.cosmega.com.

Run Search Master to open the window shown in Figure 5.4. The registered version of Search Master enables all of the search engines shown in its window. The demo version only accesses the engines in the top row. Enter your search phrase and click each of the search engines you want to use. Search Master is optimized for Netscape Navigator and will use that browser if it is installed on your system.

FIGURE 5.4 Using Search Master

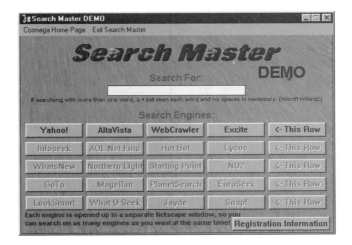

Rather than collect all of the results in one window like Copernic99, Search Master opens a separate browser window for each search engine. Open each window in turn to display the results.

MP3 Fiend

If you are interested in locating MP3 music files, then choose MP3 Fiend, a program that focuses on MP3 sites. You'll find a copy of the program on the CD, or you can download it from http://www.mp3fiend.com.

This program searches 11 MP3 engines simultaneously and lets you download MP3 files using the GetRight program, which is also on the CD. In fact, before running MP3 Fiend, install GetRight so you are prepared to download music files.

When you run MP3 Fiend, it first downloads the current list of search sites from the manufacturer's site, and then opens the window shown in Figure 5.5. Enter a search phrase, such as song name or artist, and click Begin Search. The program connects to the Internet and displays the progress of its search.

FIGURE 5.5 Using MP3 Fiend

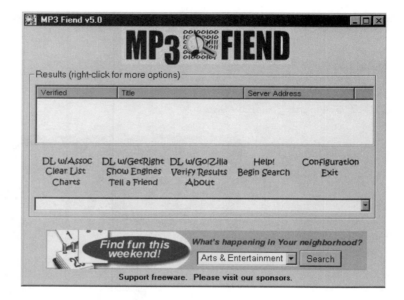

When all of the sites have been searched, click Close to display the download sites for the music files in the MP3 Fiend window, as shown in Figure 5.6. To download one of the songs, click the DL option for the downloading file you have installed.

Search By Media

To search for various types of media, such as music or video, use Search By Media, which you'll find on the CD or you can download from http://www.searchbymedia.com.

Installing the program places an icon for it in the system tray. Right-click the icon and choose Search from the menu that appears to start Search By Media, which will dial into the Internet if you are not already connected.

The Search By Media program is shown in Figure 5.7. To search based on text, click the Keywords search option button, and then enter the search phrase in the text box. To search for MP3 music, click the MP3 Search option button and enter a keyword in the associated text box.

FIGURE 5.6   Search results in MP3 Fiend

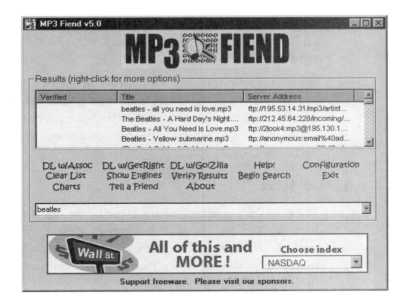

FIGURE 5.7   Search By Media

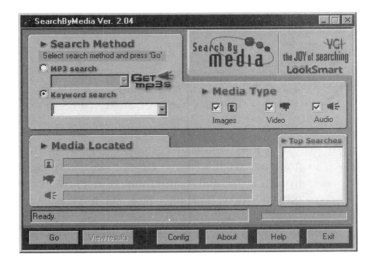

Next, select the check boxes for the type of media you are searching for—images, video, and audio. By default, the program looks for files using most of the popular file formats. Use the Config button to customize how Search By Media works.

When you're ready to search the Internet, click the Go button. If you are offline, Search By Media connects to the Internet, and begins the search. As it scans, you'll see progress bars in the Media Located section of the window, and a box may appear asking if you want to list the sites located as the search continues.

If you select Yes, the sites appear listed as links in a browser window. To see thumbnail sketches of the sites, click the link Images in the browser window, or click View Results in the Search By Media window. Click Sites in the window to return to the listing of sites, or click Audio to list located audio files.

Turbo Start

The popular search engines are just one way to locate information on the Internet. You can also search a specific Web site for information. For example, if you're looking for information about health, you can navigate to any of thousands of health-related sites and search their own database for information.

 While you'll learn about getting health, legal, and other information in later sections of this book, you can get a start by using the program Turbo Start that you'll find on the CD with this book, and which you can download from http://www.rashminsanghvi.com/turbo.

 NOTE For Turbo Start to work correctly it must be installed manually from the root directory of the CD-Rom, \TurboStart\setup.exe.

Turbo Start installs its basic Web page on your own hard disk. When the program is started, it launches your Web browser, quickly loads its Web page from your hard disk, and then connects to its own Internet site through your ISP. The Turbo Start page is shown in Figure 5.8.

Here's how to use the page to locate specific information.

1. Select a category from the list box on the left of the screen. There are a number of options in the list; some of these include Arts, Sports, Health, and Education.

2. When you choose a category, several search engines or sites appear to the right of the list.

3. Select the check boxes for all of the sites you wish to use for your search.

FIGURE 5.8 Using Turbo Start for Web searches

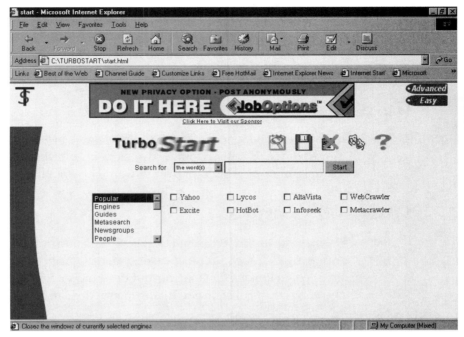

4. Enter your search words in the text box next to the Start button.

5. Pull down the list to its left and select the type of search. The options are the word(s), all the words, or the phrase.

6. Click Start.

The searches are launched in each of the selected sites; they are then opened in individual browser windows. All of the windows will be indicated on the Windows taskbar, so click each in turn and review the findings.

6 Real Men Look Up Directions

So maybe it's not as neat as the map on the screen in James Bond's Aston Martin, but you can get driving maps to any location off the Internet.

Find Out Where You're Going

Before heading off on that business trip or the drive to Grandma's house, get step-by-step directions from the Internet so you don't get lost. If you're headed for a vacation spot, get maps of the area around your hotel, or near the popular tourist locations.

Here's What You Need

All you will need is access to the Internet and a printer, if you want a hard-copy of the map. A good quality ink-jet or laser printer will have the best results, a high-quality color printer would be even better!

Sites and Features

Maps on the Internet can show a specific location or detailed point-to-point driving instructions. In most cases, you can easily switch from one to the other. When looking at a map of your destination, for example, there may be a button you can click to get driving instructions from your starting point.

NOTE If you want to get directions as you're driving, go to the computer store and ask for a GPS mapping program and receiver. With the kit and a laptop computer, you can see exactly where you are and where you have to go in real time.

There are lots of Web sites that offer maps. You'll probably find one that you like better than all of the others, and you will find that some may be more accurate than others. The driving directions may also be more general than specific—some tell you to turn off a major road where there is no exit, and a lot of the time you won't be able to find addresses in very new developments, within some industrial parks, or in some rural areas where only horses and cows graze. If you're city or suburb folks, then chances are the address you're looking for will be there.

Almost all of the maps let you zoom and navigate:

Zooming Enlarges or reduces the area being shown on the screen. Zoom out when you want to see a wide geographic area but with less detail; zoom in when you need more detail and individual street names.

Navigation   Changes the area displayed by the use of arrow buttons or compass directions. Usually the compass directions are set up so you can click the up arrow or the letter N on the compass to see what's located north of there, and so on.

Microsoft's Expedia

Microsoft's Expedia Web site is a comprehensive place to go for travel information of all types. To get a map of a location, navigate to `http://www.expediamaps.com`. You can then choose from these options:

Address Finder   Lets you see a map showing a specific street address.

Place Finder   Locates a city or tourist attraction, such as the Eiffel Tower.

Driving Directions   Shows step-by-step locations between two cities.

Travel   Accesses travel information.

For example, to get the map to a specific address, follow these steps:

1. Click Address Finder to see these options:

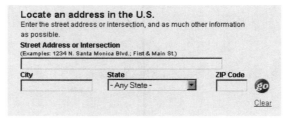

2. Enter as much information as possible to identify the location. You can either enter a street address or an intersection, such as Fifth and Main.

3. Click GO. Expedia displays a map as shown in Figure 6.1. You can zoom in or navigate through the map using the Zoom Level and Map Mover sections. You can also use the *Link*, *Print*, and *E-mail* links. If Expedia cannot find the exact location, it will display one or more similar addresses along the left of the screen. Click the address that you want to map, or click Back and try again

FIGURE 6.1 An Expedia map

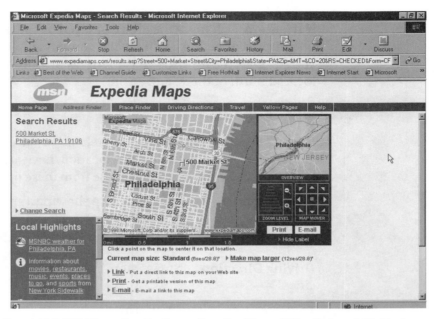

The Driving Directions option lets you specify two city names or major attractions. Enter the locations and click Go. In some cases, Expedia will ask you to refine your locations. Select the starting point and destination, and then click Go to see directions like those shown in Figure 6.2.

FIGURE 6.2 Driving directions from Expedia

Driving Directions ▸ Print

Time	Instruction	Road	Dir	For (mi)	Toward
0:00	Depart Philadelphia Airport, Pennsylvania	I-476	NW	16.1	Allentown
0:18	At I-76 Exit 28, turn left onto	I-76	W	170.2	
2:56	At I-76 Exit 12, go onto	I-70	W	152.4	Columbus
5:08	*Entering West Virginia*				
5:18	Bear left onto	I-470	W	10.3	
5:21	*Entering Ohio*				
5:28	At I-70 Exit 219, bear left onto	I-70	W	119.2	Columbus
7:20	Arrive Columbus City Hall, Ohio				

Lycos

If you want driving directions from one address to another, rather than between cities and sites, navigate to `http://www.lycos.com/roadmap.html`. Here you will be asked to fill out a form. After you are done, click Go Get It! Once the map appears, you can click a zoom level option or any of the compass directions (these appear around the map border) to navigate.

For door-to-door driving instructions, select Driving Directions from the Lycos site, or click Drive To once a map is displayed for directions to that location. In the screen that appears, enter the address from where you are starting the trip, then either enter your destination's address, or pull down the Select list to choose a site or point of interest. For example, if you need driving instructions to City Hall in Philadelphia, PA, you don't need to know its address. Pull down the Select list and choose City Halls. Then enter the city and state, and click Calculate Directions.

Select the route type, either door-to-door or city-to-city, and then one of these options:

Overview Map with Text   Shows the maps of each location with written instructions on how to get there.

Turn-by-Turn Map with Text   Shows a map for each instruction.

Text Only   Shows only the instructions without a map.

Finally, click Calculate Directions to display the driving directions.

Yahoo, Excite, and Others

All of the major search companies offer free maps and driving directions. For example, go to `http://www.yahoo.com`, click Maps, and then Driving Directions. From `http://www.excite.com`, click Maps&Directions. Then enter either an address, or enter "from" and "to" addresses within the US to get driving directions, and then click MapIt!

Some other map sites are

- ◆ `http://www3.mapsonus.com`
- ◆ `http://www.nationalgeographic.com/resources/ngo/maps`
- ◆ `http://www.mapquest.com`
- ◆ `http://www.mapblast.com/mapblast/start.hm`

7 Tracking Down Lost Souls

Want to track down your first love? Do you have a phone number but can't remember who it belongs to? Wonder who lives in that house down the street? There is a world of possibilities for finding people on the Internet.

Find an Old Friend or Relative on the Internet

Imagine having the residential and business telephone books from every city in the United States on your desk. It would be an awesome job to find a person if you didn't know where they were located. But if all that information were stored electronically so you could just enter a name to search the entire country it would be much less daunting. Wait no longer, it is on the Internet!

Here's What You Need

The only thing you will need to use this information is access to the Internet.

Sites and Features

The amazing thing about the Internet is the vast amount of information it contains. Directory sites let you search for names, addresses, and phone numbers anywhere in the United States and around the world. If you don't know a person's name, you can also do a reverse lookup. This means you can enter a phone number to see whom it belongs to or an address to see who lives there. If you find a listing that you're interested in, you can easily look up people who live in their neighborhood. There are even e-mail listings and reverse e-mail so you can match people with their e-mail addresses.

Now you won't actually find every person in the world in online directories. Unlisted telephone numbers, corporate e-mail addresses, and very new listings won't be available. But that still leaves a couple hundred million people.

AnyWho Directories

Let's start with the site `http://www.anywho.com`, where you can search for phone numbers using the interface that AT&T maintains there.

Enter the person's last name in the Last Name text box, and the zip code or city and state, and then click Search. For more options, click Advanced Search. If you're sure of the spelling leave the list next to the Last Name box set at Same As. You can also choose Sounds Like if you're not sure of the spelling or you can enter just the start of the name and choose Begins With.

Instead of entering the complete first name, it's better to enter just the first letter and leave the list set at Begins With. In some cases, the listing is under the initial and entering the full name will cause it not to be found. If you really need to enter the entire name and you are sure that is the way that it will be listed, choose Same As.

If you know the street name, city, zip code, or state, you can also enter them, but this is entirely up to you. When you're done, click Search.

If any matches are found, they will appear on-screen. If you didn't enter a state, the names are listed by state, otherwise they are in alphabetical order. Scan the list for the person you are interested in. To explore the entry you come up with, choose one of the following choices:

- ◆ Click the person's name to see the item by itself.

- ◆ Click the "vcard" icon next to the name to see details about the person's listing. Vcards are used by some e-mail, Personal Information Managers (such as Microsoft Outlook), and personal organizers to keep more detailed records of address book listings. You can learn more about vcards at `http://www.imc.org/pdi`.

- ◆ Click their street name to get a listing of people on the same street, although not necessarily on the same block.

- ◆ Click the phone number to access AT&T's ClickToDial telephone conferencing facility. You can set up a conference call for up to seven people. Calls cost 15 cents per minute within the continental U.S. Find out more about ClickToDial at `http://www.click2dial.att.com/index.html`.

- ◆ Click Maps to see a map of the address.

- ◆ Click Send Cards to send an electronic or actual card, for a fee.

- ◆ Click Send Flowers and Gifts to send a gift to the person.

NOTE The other tabs on the screen let you look up businesses, do a reverse lookup of the telephone number, and look for toll-free phone numbers, or Web sites.

AnyWho is not just an electronic version of the telephone book. It maintains its own listing of names and addresses. By clicking the Add Listing list on the left of the AnyWho window you can insert your name, address, e-mail address, and Web site address into their directory. You can also click Update Listing to modify your listing.

Along with name and address information, you can add a wish list to your AnyWho record. Click Wish List on the left of the screen to access a form for recording items you'd like for your birthday or any occasion. Click the *Update This Listing* link, and then click the Change button in the screen that appears. At the bottom of the form on the resulting page, you can enter wish list items. Persons looking at your listing can see the list by clicking the Wish List button when your item appears.

Worldwide Directories

The Internet is a worldwide phenomenon, so it should come as no surprise that you can also get telephone numbers and addresses around the globe as well.

The best place to start looking for international numbers is at `http://www.teldir.com`, which bills itself as "the Internet's original and most detailed index of online phone books."

This site not only lets you access telephone books in the United States, but also in these categories: North America and the Caribbean, South and Central America, Africa, Europe, Asia and the Middle East, and Australasia and the Pacific.

Click the link for the area or country that you are interested in to display additional links for specific phone books.

Reverse Lookups

A reverse lookup is just the opposite of a regular search. Instead of entering a name to find an address or telephone number, you enter a telephone number or address to locate the name and other information.

Reverse lookups are great, especially if you have a telephone number but you don't know to whom it belongs. It could be on a piece of paper you found in your pocket, part of an itemized listing on your telephone bill, or a number left on your pager or caller ID box.

You can also use reverse lookups to find who lives where. Perhaps you're concerned that you cannot contact an elderly friend or relative and want to contact their neighbor. Or, perhaps you're just curious about who lives in that spooky mansion at the end of the street.

The AnyWho site provides a reverse lookup by telephone number. For more reverse options, go to `http://in-123.infospace.com/_1_86314753__info .wnet/reverse.htm`.

This site lets you search by telephone number, address, or even e-mail address. There is even a reverse area code lookup that lists the geographic area covered by an area code, which is useful before making a long distance call.

Lookups of e-mail address, reverse or regular, do not catch a lot of people. Reverse lookups are more effective: you can try locating who belongs to an e-mail. If you just enter the domain, such as `@sybex.com`, you'll get a list of people at that domain who are also in the service's directory.

When All Else Fails

If you can't find the person you are looking for using directories, there are still things you can try that might work.

◆ Try doing a regular Web search. Chances are your ISP offers a search box on its home page, or you can try any of the popular search engines. You never know if the person you're looking for is famous, infamous, or otherwise did something to get their name on the Web.

◆ If you know what school they graduated from, try finding the school home page and looking for an alumni list. There may even be a link to contact the alumni association.

◆ If you know the person's occupation or employer, do a business lookup. Most of the directory services let you look up a business by name, location, or category.

◆ Do you know what the person is interested in? Try looking at Internet newsgroups.

8 Find a Job Online!

If you are independently wealthy, or plan to inherit a fortune, then you can skip this information. But if you're like the rest of us working stiffs, take a look at how you can find a better job.

Fill Those Vacant Shows!

The local newspaper and the employment office are great places to start looking for work, but real careers can be made on the Internet. Since the Internet spans the world, you can make contacts and locate job openings that are not advertised in your local newspaper.

Here's What You Need

All you need is access to the Internet, although a resume wouldn't hurt.

Sites and Features

There are actually lots of places to find work on the Internet. First, try the Web sites of companies that you'd like to work for. Most of the larger companies have links on their home pages for employment information. Clicking one of those links might take you to a listing of jobs, a place to send your resume electronically, or just a description of how to apply for work. It is a great place to start because you can target your search toward specific companies for which you'd like to work.

Instead of aiming for specific companies, you can also link up with a job-placement service. Two of the most popular on the Internet are `http://www.jobs.com` and `http://www.monster.com`.

With Jobs.com, you can download a free copy of a program called Resumail Resume. Use this program to write your resume and cover letter, which you submit to the jobs.com resume bank for forwarding to perspective employers.

At the Jobs.com Web site, you can search for jobs by city and by category. When you find a job you're interested in, click the Resumail It button to submit your resume.

At monster.com—a rather funky name for a great service listing over 170,000 jobs from more than 30,000 employers—you can find a listing of jobs as easily as entering one or more keywords into a box and clicking Go. You can also search by location or category. The resulting list of jobs shows the posting date, location, job title, and company.

You can also start your search in one of nine Career Zones: Campus, Mid-Career, Executive, Independent, Professional, International, Technology, Healthcare, and HR. Use one of these zones to track down a job at a certain level or in a specific industry.

The job titles in listings are links—click the title to read details about the offering and how to apply, and then click Apply Online to send off your resume.

The site makes it easy to apply because you can create and store your resume and cover letter on their Web site. You sign up for a free account by just entering your e-mail address. A private username and password will be e-mailed to you, usually within minutes.

Then from the Web site, click My Monster and enter your name and password to access options for storing your resume and cover letter, tracking job offers, and joining online chats.

From the My Monster screen, for example, click the Submit Resume link for an online resume form. The form includes sections for your contact and relocation information, the type of job you're looking for, compensation requirements, and educational background. At the end of the form is a large text box in which you can enter or paste the body of your resume. In fact, you should prepare your resume beforehand and then copy and paste it into the form.

In a similar manner, you can create and store a cover letter from My Monster. The letter and resume will be sent when you click Apply Online from any listed position.

If you prefer going out to get a job, use the Internet to locate job fairs in your area at http://dir.yahoo.com/Business_and_Economy/Employment_and_ Work/Jobs/Job_Fairs. In fact, Yahoo and other search engines offer a wide range of career information. At `http://careers.yahoo.com`, for example, you can find many career links.

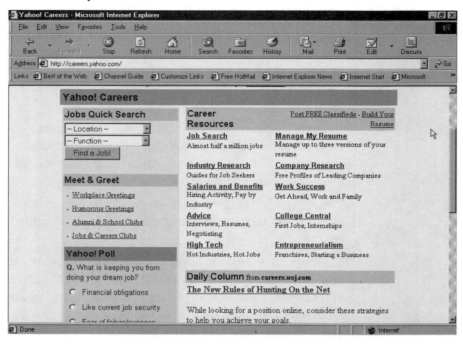

Other sources of employment information can be found at these sites:

◆ `http://www.careerpath.com`

◆ `http://www.hotjobs.com`

◆ `http://www.jobbankusa.com`

◆ `http://www.jobsearch.org`

◆ `http://www.jobweb.com`

9 Need a Roof over Your Head?

Locating the right apartment, house, condo, or co-op can be hard on the legs, wallet, and ego. Start your search for living arrangements on the

Internet, where plenty of options abound, whether you're moving around the corner or around the world.

Find a Place to Call Home

There are millions of homes for sale and apartments for rent every day. Looking through the newspaper, banging on doors, and calling realtors are just some ways to find a place to live. But you can also search for living space stress-free from the comfort of a computer.

Here's What You Need

All you will need is access to the Internet...until you find your new home, that is!

Sites and Features

The housing market is good or bad. Rates are high or low. Money is tight or loose. There are lots of reasons why finding the right place to live can be difficult, but the Internet can help you find a home and a mortgage to pay for it.

NOTE At `http://www.jobs.com`, click the Local Realty button for housing information.

Getting Approved

If you want to make sure you can afford a new home before you look for one, prequalify for a mortgage or, better still, get pre-approved.

Prequalification means that you can afford a home up to a certain price and indicates to the seller that you should have no problem getting a mortgage. The prequalification, however, is not a commitment from a lender. Pre-approval, on the other hand, means that a lender has actually committed to giving you a mortgage for a certain amount, even though you have not yet picked out a specific property.

Some places to prequalify, get pre-approval, and apply for loans are

◆ `http://www.eloan.com`

- http://www.iown.com
- http://www.quickenmortgage.com

You can prequalify at a local bank, of course, but you can also do it online by filling in a form requesting some basic financial information. After filling in the form at http://www.eloan.com, for example, you'll learn if you can afford that dream house.

One company, Quickenmortgage (http://www.quickenmortgage.com), even creates a letter stating that you are prequalified for a certain loan amount that you can print and take with you to a meeting with the seller.

To get pre-approved, you have to enter more detailed information, basically applying for the loan. With a pre-approval letter in hand you may be able to strike a better deal.

NOTE Prequalification does not obligate you or the online company to actually establish a loan together. The prequalification is based entirely on your responses to the online form. The lender does not validate your responses until you ask to be pre-approved or actually apply for the loan.

Finding Your Home

Once you know what you can afford, you have to find a home in that price range. For that, the multiple listing was a great invention. By entering a house with the Multiple Listing Service (MLS) a realtor can offer a house to every realtor and prospective buyer in the United States. So if you're looking for a home, the first place to start is at http://www.realtors.com. With almost one and half million listings from the MLS, the site offers the widest range of homes available, including condos and co-ops. You can choose homes by the geographic area, price, size, and many other criteria to narrow down your search.

When you find a good prospect, print a copy of the MLS listing, which usually includes a photograph of the property and detailed description. Take the printout to a local realtor, or just drive by the house to check it out. If you need to find a local realtor, http://www.realtor.com can help with that too.

Another excellent source is http://www.homescout.com. This site includes many MLS as well as non-MLS listings. It also includes a search engine for loans, where you can shop for mortgages.

If you're just looking for a roommate to share expenses, then there are some other great sites. Try these to match up with someone compatible:

- ◆ http://www.e-roommate.com
- ◆ http://www.roommate-assistant.com
- ◆ http://www.roomateservice.com
- ◆ http://www.roommatelocator.com

While some companies list roommates throughout the United States, Roommate Express (http://www.e-roommate.com) specializes in those West Coast areas where housing is at a premium.

10 Hi. What's Your Sign?

Before you dust off those platform shoes or get the wrinkles out of your leisure suit for a happening night on the town, consider making contact over the Internet.

Finding a Date

If you thought finding a job and a place to live could be difficult, how about finding a pleasant, compatible person to spend some time with? Finding a date, friend, or companion is not so easy these days. Sometimes it seems like all the right folks are already taken.

Here's What You Need

All you will need to try out these opportunities is access to the Internet, and a free Saturday night.

Sites and Features

There are a whole lot of places to find a date over the Internet. You can try chat rooms, the online equivalent to the local watering hole. The chat rooms in AOL, CompuServe, or some other ISP can be fun and socially rewarding, as long as you use some common sense and caution. Who you are talking to in a chat room may be a mystery.

For a more structured and formal way to meet people, you can try going through online dating services. They work about the same way as other dating services, except you swap information online.

The service at `http://www.one-and-only.com` lets you place one free ad before signing on. Check out `http://www.matchamerica.com` for a nation-wide dating service, or `http://www.1stclassdating.com` to start looking.

If you are looking for a how-to on dating, rather than a direct match, try `http://www.fayez.simplenet.com/romanceguide.htm`, which calls itself the "ultimate multimedia guide to flirting, dating, love, and romance." You can also learn the scientific method for finding a date at `http://pc65.frontier.osrhe.edu/hs/science/hsimeth/htm`.

If you want more than a date, you can try match-making services, such as these:

- ◆ `http://www.findmymate.com`
- ◆ `http://www.match.com`
- ◆ `http://meetamate.com`

Or for something really different, try `http://www.williedaly.com` where a horse whisperer offers matchmaking hints while you go horseback riding in Ireland.

It's About Time

When someone came up with the expression "Time is Money," the Internet wasn't around, but the saying certainly applies to the Internet too. The Internet can not only charge you for time, but it can also take up your time, save you time, and even tell you the time. In this part of the book, we'll look at interesting connections between time and the Internet.

11 Synchronize Your Watches

Does every clock in your home have a different time? Well, spread throughout this planet are timeservers—computers that have the exact time—or as exact as humanly possible.

Use the Internet to Synchronize Your Clocks

The good folks at these timeservers let you synchronize your computer's clock to theirs. You can log on to the Internet and automatically set your computer clock to the exact time.

Here's What You Need

All you will need is a shareware or freeware program that you can download from the Internet. You'll find several of them on the CD with this book, including EZE Clock, YATS32, and CMDTime.

Sites and Features

Using free or inexpensive software, which you can find on the CD or download over the Internet, you can automatically update your computer's clock to the second. If time is that important to you, run one of these programs periodically to keep your clock current. Some programs give you the option of setting your clock each time you connect to the Internet or even when you start your computer.

There are scores of programs that automatically get the current time and update your system clock.

EZE Clock

EZE Clock is one example. This shareware program displays a digital clock on your desktop that you can customize. The program checks in with the National Institute of Standards Timeserver every time you start your dialup connection to access the Internet and updates your system clock as needed. You can find EZE Clock on the CD included with this book, or by downloading it from http://www.atssoftware.com. You control EZE Clock by right clicking it to display these options.

Date/Time Properties   Opens Windows' Date/Time Properties window.

Run as Service   Runs EZE Clock every time you start your computer.

Select ISP   Dials your ISP when you manually tell it to synch the time.

Display Clock   Toggles between displaying clock on the desktop and making the icon invisible.

Keep Clock on Top   Displays the clock above all open windows.

Clock Colors   Sets the foreground and background colors.

Enable Sys Tray Icon   Places an icon for EZE Clock in the system tray.

Set Time Now   Dials into the NIST timeserver and sets your clock.

View Log   Displays a text file showing EZE clock actions.

Help   Opens the EZE Clock help system.

About   Gives you version and registration information.

Close EZE Clock   Closes the program and removes the clock from the screen.

YATS32

YATS32 is another time synch program provided on the accompanying CD. You can also download it from http://www.dillobits.com.

When you start the program, you have to either choose to evaluate it or register it. The Evaluate options lets you run it free for a limited time, the Register option allows you to purchase it. If you run YATS32, you will see the following dialog box, which displays several default timeservers, as shown in Figure 11.1.

FIGURE 11.1   Setting your clock with YATS32

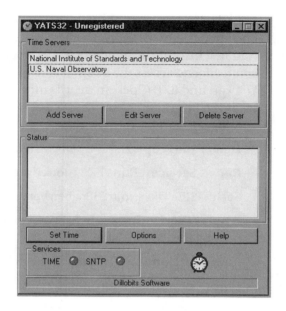

Click the timeserver you want to use and then click Set Time. The program dials into your ISP and sets your clock. The results will appear in the dialog box.

You can select additional timeservers using the Add Server button. The Options button lets you customize YATS32. You have a choice of several options that will run YATS32 each time you connect to the Internet or whenever you start your computer.

CMDTime

If you are uncomfortable with programs that take control and appear automatically, you can synch your clock using the command line program CMDTime. This program is on the CD and can be found at http://www .softshape.com.

You run CMDTime from the command line—from the Start ➤ Run option on the desktop or from the MS-DOS Prompt. Command options give you the choice of a quick adjustment based on three timeservers or a precise adjustment based on ten. They recommend using ten servers if you have a poor connection that might delay the process.

From the Start ➤ Run menu, enter any of the following commands, which assume the program is in the root directory of the C: drive:

C:/cmdTime /? Shows how to use CMDTime.

C:/cmdTime /Q Performs a quick adjustment using three timeservers.

C:/cmdTime /P Performs a precise adjustment using ten timeservers.

C:/cmdTime /Q +XX Adds *xx* minutes to the time.

C:/cmdTime /Q –XX Subtracts *xx* minutes from the time.

C:/cmdTime /T Shows the server response time.

C:/cmdTime server Performs an adjustment using the timeserver listed—you can list up to 10.

After you select one of the above commands, the program dials into your ISP if you are not already connected, gets the time, and sets your date and time based on your time zone.

More Timeservers

Here are a few other URLs and locations of popular timeservers. To use one of these, enter it following the C:/cmd, as in C:/cmd/black-ice.cc.vt.edu.

WEB SITE	LOCATION
black-ice.cc.vt.edu	Virginia Tech Computing Center, Blacksburg, VA
chime.utoronto.ca	University of Toronto, Ontario, Canada
churchy.udel.edu	University of Delaware, Newark, DE
clock.psu.edu	Penn State University, University Park, PA

12 Tracking Time Spent Online

As one who knows can tell you, the Internet can become addictive. Before you know it, the sun is shining, you've had no sleep, and you're already late for work.

Preventing Family Trouble

If "Honey, come to bed already" is a familiar mating call in your household, then maybe you need to keep track of your time online. If you want to save your marriage, family, or job, read on....

Here's What You Need

For this essay you won't need much of anything. You may find some useful free or inexpensive software on the CD or available for download from the Internet, however.

Sites and Features

With all of the wonderful features you are learning about in this book, you may be spending more time than you want online. It is not your fault. It is easy to lose track of time. But spending too much time online can break up a relationship, cause family strife, exceed your credit card limits, and make the phone company too happy.

For help in exercising some control over yourself and others in your household, keep track of your time online. The easiest way to do this is to watch the clock in the Windows system tray, on your wrist, or on the wall. This method doesn't cost anything or require any software; it only requires some discipline.

If you need some additional help, check to see if your ISP has a feature for tracking your online time. If they do, you can check you online time regularly to see how close you're getting to—or how far away you are from—your limit of free hours.

If discipline is what you lack, consider some free or inexpensive alternatives. Several programs for tracking your online time are included on the accompanying CD, and there are plenty more that you can download from the Internet.

Online Time

One such program, Online Time, is on the CD and can be downloaded from `http://users.forthnet.gr/the/lonewolf/s`. Online Time displays an icon (a yellow face) in the system tray—the area of the Windows taskbar where you'll see the time. This icon indicates when you are on and offline. Point to the icon to see the length of time online.

You can also click the icon to open the program window. The window shows the current time, the length of the current session, the length of your longest session, and your total online time. It also displays the number of connections, the number of times you ran the program, the date you installed it, and your system's IP address. You can reset the settings by clicking the Reset icon.

Minimize the window to return it to the icon in the system tray. If you don't like the icon, you can right-click it and choose Icons from the menu to select a new one.

Modem Logger

For a more robust way of tracking your time, try Modem Logger. This program is also on the CD, and it can be downloaded from `http://come.to/ kiryssoft`.

As you can see from the Modem Logger window shown in Figure 12.1, the program shows the current session time, the length you've been online during the current day, and your total online time.

FIGURE 12.1   Tracking online time with Modem Logger

Using the Options menu, you can associate your browser or e-mail program as the timer "client." You can then run the program and start timing by clicking Options and choosing Run Client.

One nice feature of Modem Logger is its cost log. If you pay for your online time in either ISP or phone-company charges, you can keep track of charges you have accrued. Choose Cost Logging Preferences from the Options menu to open a window, as shown in Figure 12.2. The window in this figure shows what this setup would look like for British Telecom in the United Kingdom. This company charges by the minute. By setting the cost configuration, you can keep track of how much your online time is costing. By using the Auto-configure option, you can have Modem Logger enter the information for the most popular telephone services for you.

FIGURE 12.2 Calculating online costs

Days	From	To	S.C.C.	Intermediate cost			Normal cost		
				Delay	Unit	Unit Cost	Delay	Unit	Unit Cost
All ▼	06.00	18.00	0.05	0	0	0.00	75	60	0.04
All ▼	18.00	06.00	0.05	0	0	0.00	150	60	2.00
Fri ▼	18.00	24.00	0.05	0	0	0.00	300	60	0.01
Sat ▼	00.00	24.00	0.05	0	0	0.00	300	60	0.01
Sun ▼	00.00	24.00	0.05	0	0	0.00	300	60	0.01
Mon ▼	00.00	06.00	0.05	0	0	0.00	300	60	0.01
None ▼	00.00	00.00	0.00	0	0	0.00	0	0	0.00
None ▼	00.00	00.00	0.00	0	0	0.00	0	0	0.00
None ▼	00.00	00.00	0.00	0	0	0.00	0	0	0.00
None ▼	00.00	00.00	0.00	0	0	0.00	0	0	0.00

Cost Configuration — Time Grid. [Autoconfigure] [Ok] [Help] [Cancel]

WinAnalyzer

A program that goes a few steps further to help you control your online time is WinAnalyzer. You'll find this product on the CD. This program not only tracks your online time and cost, but can check your e-mail and synchronize your system time. It can also be set to dial in at a specific time or hang up at a certain time. When WinAnalyzer is installed, an icon is installed in the system tray. When you open WinAnalyzer by clicking this icon, you will see a menu bar along the left side and eight command buttons. Use these to work the program.

You can right-click the icon on the system tray to access configuration options.

By combining settings, you can use WinAnalyzer to dial in, check your mail, and then hang up. Follow the steps below to configure the program and dial your ISP to check your mail.

1. Right-click the WinAnalyzer icon in the system tray and choose Configuration ➢ Connection.

2. In the box that appears, click the dial-up networking connection you want to use, and then click Set as Default.

3. Click the Advanced button in the dialog box.

4. In the box that appears, enter your user name and password, and then click OK.

5. Click Hide.

6. Right-click the icon and choose Configuration ➤ E-mail Watch to open the Preferences dialog box.

7. Enable the check box labeled Check E-mail Immediately Upon Connection.

8. Enter your user name, e-mail password, and the address of your mail server.

9. Click Connection on the left of the box.

10. In the box that appears, pull down the Action menu and choose Auto Hangup.

11. Set the inactivity period to 5 minutes.

12. Select the option Redial Until Connected.

13. Click OK.

14. Right-click the icon and choose Configuration ➤ Timer.

15. Enable the Start Dialing At Time option and set the time you want the program to check your e-mail.

16. Click Start Dialup Sequence.

Now leave your computer just the way it is—go out for the evening or get a good night's sleep. At the time you set, WinAnalyzer will call your ISP (redialing if the line is busy), check your e-mail, wait five minutes, and then hang up.

General Timers

If you're interested in the overall time that you're on your computer, not just online, use a more general timing program.

TimeIt!   TimeIt! lets you turn on and off the time and it allows you to set an alarm. If you only want to go online for 30 minutes, for example, set the alarm for 30 minutes, click the Start button, and then connect to the Internet. Log off when you hear the alarm. TimeIt! is on the CD and can be downloaded from `http://members.1stconnect.com/geneg/duquesne_softworks.htm`.

Total Timer   Total Timer differs from TimeIt! in the following manner. It just tells you how long your computer has been on and does not use Internet time at all. It is a quick alternative when you want to monitor your computer usage time. Total Timer is on the CD and can be downloaded from the collection of software at http://www.winfiles.com.

13 Understanding Time Zones

"Hello, sorry to wake you, but I'm selling…..".

Doing business internationally, or bicoastally, is great, but don't jeopardize that deal by calling a client in the middle of their night. People get very angry when their pleasant sleep is interrupted by a sales call. Of course, if you do wake the client up, you can always pretend to be a competitor.

Following Time Zone Netiquette

Consider the time zone when using online chats too. Online chats are great for meeting new people, but don't expect a buddy from across the globe to stay up all night to talk to you. Make sure you know what time it is before making that online or long-distance call.

Here's What You Need

The only things you will need are an Internet connection, and some handy software that you can find either on the accompanying CD or for download on the Internet.

You should also understand what *Greenwich Mean Time (GMT)* is. Because Internet services don't really know where you are, they show the time in GMT, the current time in Greenwich, England. (Go figure!) GMT is a standard way to reference time regardless of location, and it is used to coordinate all sorts of worldwide activities.

Web sites refer to times in other locations as either the actual local time or in relation to GMT. The notation +2, for example, would mean two hours past the GMT displayed. So if the GMT is shown as 16:24, and your time is referenced as +2, then it is 18:24 at your location.

Now what the heck is 18:24? I forgot to mention that GMT uses a 24-hour clock format. Instead of counting from 11 A.M., 12 noon, 1 P.M., 2 P.M., and so on, it counts 11:00, 12:00, 13:00, 14:00, etc. To convert from a 24-hour clock to a 12-hour clock, just subtract 12. This makes 18:24 exactly 6:24 P.M. Times smaller than 12:00 are A.M.; times greater than 12:00 are P.M.

Sites and Features

Before looking for that chat buddy online, or making that long distance call, check out the local time for the person you are trying to reach. You can do so online or by running a program on your computer.

If you're online, or plan to go online, check either of these sites: `http://www.worldtime.com`, or `http://www.businesswindow.com`.

WORLDTIME

WORLDTIME is a free service that lets you select the location by either clicking the globe or choosing from a list of cities. Once you get to `http://www.worldtime.com`, click the link *Access The Service's Main Page* to see the site shown in Figure 13.1.

FIGURE 13.1   **Global time at WORLDTIME**

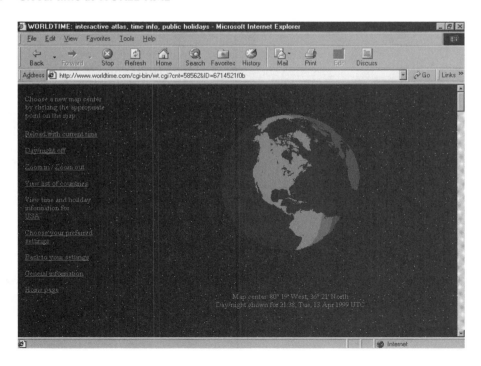

Click the part of the globe that you want to center in the window—you may have to click several times to rotate the globe to the correct location. The centerpoint is the portion of the globe that is used to determine the time in this program; the time will be shown below the globe. The globe will also be shaded to indicate day and night.

You can perform these functions using the links on the left of the site:

- ◆ Refresh the page to indicate the current time.
- ◆ Turn the day/night indicator off or on.
- ◆ Zoom in and out of the graphic.
- ◆ Display a list of countries that can be used as the map centerpoint.
- ◆ Show the specific time in major cities—this is useful for countries with several time zones.
- ◆ Customize the way the globe appears.
- ◆ Quickly change to your custom settings.
- ◆ Get general information on WORLDTIME.
- ◆ Jump to the WORLDTIME home page.

BusinessWindow

BusinessWindow handles the time differently. This site is a subscription service for members, but it provides a free timetable for many major cities around the world. From the site's home page (http://www .businesswindow.com), choose World Time from the left-hand pane of the screen. From the next screen, choose an option from the World Time for Non Paying Members section.

You can choose to display a list of countries alphabetically, or by zone in relation to GMT. For each location, you'll see the local time as well as the offset from GMT. So, when it is 16:19 GMT, it is already 20:19 (or 8:19 p.m) in Kabul, Afghanistan—well after the end of the office day!

World Time Software

Rather than go online to get the time in various locations, you can download a number of programs from various places on the Internet, and then display the time offline. There are scores of such programs, including World Clocks, GTime, and WorldTime2.

World Clocks   You'll find World Clocks on the CD with this book. World Clocks lets you display any number of clocks on-screen, each displaying a different time zone, and each showing the location's actual time, not GMT.

So consider using World Clocks to display the time for each chat buddy or your major overseas clients.

The first time you run World Clocks, you should configure the clock by right clicking on the clock and choosing Configure. The default setting shows the city, the date, and the offset from GMT. You can modify the caption that appears with the clock and change its foreground and background colors. If you do not want the GMT time to appear in the caption, for example, delete the characters ($GMT), which tell the program to place the GMT time on your screen.

Use the Clock Adjust tab to configure the clock for Daylight Savings Time. Use the General tab to choose a 24-hour format and to show the seconds. Click OK when you're done to display the clock.

To add one or more additional time zones, follow these steps:

1. Right-click the displayed clock and choose New from the shortcut menu. A duplicate clock appears.

2. Right-click one of the duplicates and choose Configure to open the Configure Clock dialog box.

3. Select the city or time zone and then click OK.

You can remove a clock from the screen by right-clicking and choosing Close. Select Exit from the shortcut menu to stop World Clocks, and to remove the icon from the system tray. World Clocks stores the clock configuration in your computer's registry, so the same time zones appear the next time you start the program.

GTime and WorldTime2   The programs GTime and WorldTime2 take a different approach. They let you display a list of people and where they are located; these programs also display a local time for each location. In order to make these entries, you must already know the difference between your time and the locations you want to add. After these are added, all you will need to do is glance at the list you've created before looking for a chat buddy or making a long distance call.

You'll fine GTime on the CD, or you can download it from `http://users.forthnet.gr/the/lonewolf/s`.

GTime lets you keep track of time in different locations in relation to your own time, instead of GMT, but you still have to use a 24-hour clock. The program starts with a blank window to which you add the locations you are interested in. From the GTime window, click Add to see a dialog box similar to this one:

Enter the location and name of the person at that location; also adjust the difference between your time and theirs (the difference is measure in 30-minute intervals—before(-) and after(+) your own time). For example, suppose you're in New York and your client is in London, which is five hours ahead in time. Enter London in the Location box, and the client's name in the Name box. Make sure the Difference in Minutes is set at +, and advanced the time to 300.

When you click Save, the locations will appear in the GTime window. You'll see the difference between the two locations, and the current time and date in each location. If you want to add locations, all of the information will be computed for these as well.

Use the buttons in the program's toolbar to modify or delete a listing, or to resize the window. If you find a monthly calendar useful, click the calendar icon. The calendar also shows the number of the week (with weeks numbered 1-52 beginning in January), and you can use the scroll bar to display other months. Click OK in the calendar window to close it.

Use the Notes icon in the toolbar to open a notepad-like window for recording reminders and other text. The text is saved in a file called Notes that opens whenever you click the Note icon. You can also open the file from your desktop using Notepad or any word processing program.

WorldTime2 is also on the CD and can be downloaded from `http://www.molecular-software.com`.

The WorldTime2 window, along with its List Management dialog box is shown in Figure 13.2. Click List Management inWorldTime2 to add and remove people from the list.

FIGURE 13.2 WorldTime2

To add a person, follow these steps:

1. Click List Management in WorldTime2.

2. Click Add. The notation <NewPerson> appears in the People list.

3. Enter the person's name in the Name text box. It is echoed in the People list.

4. Enter the location in the Location text box.

5. Set the number of hours and minutes of time difference.

6. Select Ahead or Behind, as appropriate. The time at that location appears at the Their Time prompt.

7. Click Close.

WorldTime2 keeps the clock running in the list even if the window is mini- mized. To customize how the program works, click Options. In the dialog box that appears, you can set how often the time is updated (up to 60 sec- onds) when the application is open or minimized. You can also choose to keep the window in the foreground, and you can save its position so it reappears in the foreground each time it is opened.

14 Stay on Time and on Schedule

Never get caught off guard again without your trusty date book or calendar. You can use FREE services to maintain your schedule online and keep track of appointments, meetings, and other events.

Keep Your Schedule Updated Online

Staying coordinated is not always an easy task—that's why calendars, date books, handheld computers, and personal information managers (PIMs) are so popular these days. If you have one of those small handheld devices, you can easily carry it with you to check or arrange appointments and look up addresses. You can also get PIM software, such as Microsoft Outlook, for use on laptops and desktop PCs, or you can do it all online.

Here's What You Need

All you need to maintain a schedule online is a connection to the Internet and free registration with an online calendar service.

Sites and Features

PIMs are great for the busy executive, or anyone who has a busy schedule, a list of contacts, or a to-do list to maintain. If you move around a lot and work at a number of different computers, it is difficult to keep all of the information up-to-date and synchronized. You might schedule a meeting on your laptop, forget to update the data in your desktop, and then miss the meeting because you're reviewing your schedule on the office computer.

A solution to this dilemma is to use a free, Web-based PIM. That's right—your schedule and address book can be maintained on the service's own computer rather than your laptop or desktop. You can check your schedule, make appointments, and keep an address book from any computer that has access to the Internet. Some of the services even let you synchronize the online data with your own computer; you can then synchronize your schedule with a handheld device, such as a Palm Pilot, Casseopia, or other Windows Consumer Electronics (CE) devices.

While the features vary, some of the online services include the following:

Calendaring Lets you maintain your appointment schedule online. You can even share it with others to arrange meetings and you can check the schedules of participants for free time.

Task List Keeps a list of activities you have to perform and of your progress performing them.

Address Book Maintains name, address, e-mail, and other information about contacts, customers, and colleagues.

Free E-mail Gives you an e-mail address for sending and receiving messages.

File Storage Lets you upload documents and other files for safekeeping to the service's computer. Use this service to keep files handy for access from any Internet computer, to share files with others, or to back up important files.

Personal Web Sites Give you space for a home page.

Bookmark Management Lets you maintain a list of favorites or bookmarked sites for easy access from any Internet computer.

Synchronizing Lets you update your files so your Web-based PIM and your laptop, desktop, or handheld computer have the most current information.

There are dozens of free PIMs on the Internet. All of these services make you register the first time you use them, but the basic services are free. The only problem with these services being free is that the only way they can afford to be so is by advertising.

One other problem of Web-based PIMs is speed. It takes longer to log on to the Internet, sign on to the PIM site and check your calendar than it does to just open your notebook and check with Microsoft Outlook or some other program. Still, Web-based PIMs can be great resources if you're on the go and hopping from one computer to another.

Because of their popularity, new PIMs are popping up all of the time, while some current ones may be folding due to the competition. In this chapter, we'll look at several that offer a wide range of services and which—as of this writing—have been around awhile.

VISTO

One of my favorite Web-based PIMs is Visto, a free service you can find at `http://www.visto.com`. Signing up is easy, just fill in an on-screen form with some basic information and choose a password.

In addition to calendaring and an address book, Visto lets you upload files for storage and helps you organize them into folders. You can also maintain a to-do list and organize bookmarks for navigating the Internet. Visto also provides group folders and home pages.

Once you register and logon to Visto, you'll see the choices shown in Figure 14.1. The tabs along the top of the window and the options down the left side provide access to Visto's main functions. Registering for Visto also gives you an e-mail account, as in alan@`visto.com`. The e-mail page lets you access your Visto e-mail in order to send and receive messages and files.

FIGURE 14.1   **The main Visto window**

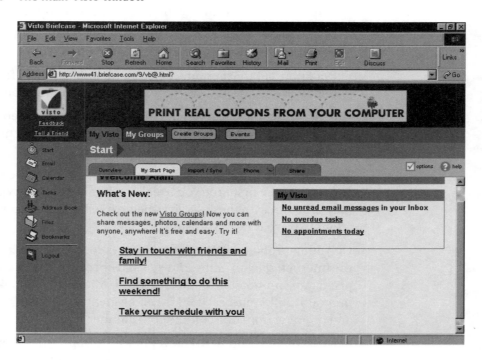

The Files area lets you store documents, graphics, and other files on Visto's computer. You can access the files from any Internet connection and share them with other users by specifying a password for them to use. The Files page lets you upload and download files, and create folders in which you can organize them.

Use the address book to store e-mail addresses that you frequently access. Then it will be easy to use the address book to look up people to invite to meetings and to share files with. The address book works just like most computer address books; it lets you add, edit, and delete contacts.

The bookmark page lets you organize your favorite sites, much like Favorites in Microsoft Internet Explorer and bookmarks in Netscape Navigator. You add the addresses of sites that you want to access, and can organize them into groups. By storing your bookmarks online, you can access the sites from any Internet connection.

Because calendaring and maintaining task lists are elements in most PIMs, lets look at these in a little more detail.

The Calendar   The heart of all PIMs, Web-based or otherwise, is the calendar. You use the calendar to schedule both appointments and meetings, and to make sure you don't forget them. Web-based PIMs let you share your calendar with others; this way you can plan group meetings, parties, and other events and also check and make sure all of the participants are available.

Once you are in the Calendar screen, use the arrows next to the date to change the date shown, or click a date in the miniature monthly calendars on the right. You can always click the Today button to return to the current day.

You can add an appointment to the calendar in one of two ways.

◆ Click the New button to create an appointment in which you designate the date and time.

◆ Click the underlined time in the calendar window to create an appointment for that day and time.

In both cases, the appointment window appears. From this screen you enter the details of the appointment and invite others to attend. You can also edit a document you have already created by changing the day, time, or length of the appointment. After you have made any changes to the appointment, click the Attendees button to invite others from your Visto address book.

When you click OK, your appointment appears in the calendar. Use the check box to indicate when the appointment is completed, or click the appointment to edit it.

NOTE Use the Share Calendar button to designate other users who can have access to your calendar.

Task List Chances are you have a "to-do list" somewhere around your home or office. Web-based PIMs let you maintain this list on their Web site so you can track your progress, and let you see which tasks are behind schedule, on schedule, and completed.

Click Tasks in the left of the Visto window to open the task list showing all current tasks.

To insert a new task, follow these steps.

1. Click New in the Task list to open the window, shown in Figure 14.2.

FIGURE 14.2 Creating a task

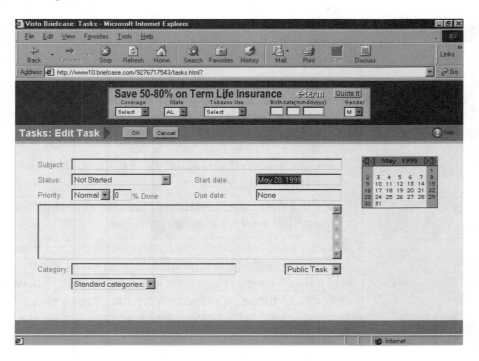

2. Enter the subject of the task as well as its start and due dates (if it has these).

3. Use the Status list to mark the task as Not started, In progress, Completed, Waiting on someone else, or Deferred.

4. Pull down the Priority list and choose High, Normal, or Low.

5. If you've already started the task, enter the percentage complete in the % Done text box.

6. In the large text box, enter a description of the task.

7. Type a category for the task, or pull down the Standard Categories list and choose one of the built-in categories.

8. Designate the task as Public or Private.

9. Click OK.

You can review all tasks in the main Task window, and glance at which are complete, which are in progress, and which are overdue.

Visto Groups   A *group* can be any number of persons with which you want to share information, messages, and files. In a way, setting up a group is like creating a personal Web site. You can create a group for family members, friends, or business associates. Each group has a message area for posting and replying to messages, file storage, and a common calendar. As the group manager, you create the group and invite others to join. You also establish a password that members must enter to access the group.

To create a group, follow these steps:

1. Connect to `http://www.visto.com`, enter your user name and password, and click Log In to Visto.

2. Click Create Groups to start a series of screens in which you enter information and select options.

3. In the first screen, just read the information and click the Next button.

4. In the second screen, enter a name for the group, a one-line description, and an optional message that you want to appear on the group homepage. Click Next.

5. In the third screen, enter a password that members must have to access the group, then specify the time zone to use for the group calendar. Click Next twice.

6. You can now choose to upload a graphic from your disk to display on the home page, choose to allow members to change the content of the home page, and add another URL as a link.

7. Click Next and then Finish.

8. You can now invite others to join the group. In the To box, enter the e-mail addresses of the people you want to join the group. Add the password to the text of the message, and then click Send. Each invited member receives an e-mail inviting them to join; each message should also contain a link to the group page.

When you log in to Visto, the names of your groups should appear with the other tabs. From these tabs, you and other group members can post and reply to messages, check the calendar for group events, and access shared files.

AnyDay

You can find AnyDay, another powerful Web-based PIM, at `http://www.anyday.com`. Registration is quick and easy. Just enter some basic information and then log on with your user name and password to access a calendar, as shown in Figure 14.3.

FIGURE 14.3   **The AnyDay calendar**

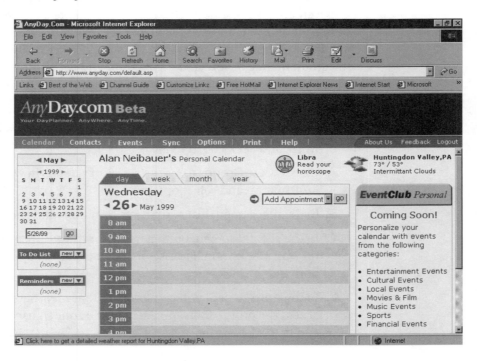

AnyDay provides your horoscope and the local weather (by using your registration information); it also offers a calendar, a to-do list, and a reminder list. To navigate in the calendar view, either use the tabs on the calendar to change between the day, week, month, or yearly view, or use the small monthly calendar on the left to change dates.

To add an appointment to the calendar, click the date of the appointment to display the appointment form. Other options further down the form let you add e-mail addresses (of others you want to invite to the meetings), designate your preferred type of appointment reminder, and set up recurring appointments on your calendar.

The reminder options let you either choose to display a reminder in a box when you log on to AnyDay, or have an e-mail reminder sent to you at a designated amount of time before the appointment.

The Repeat Appointment options let you designate how often the event occurs and when the appointment stops reoccurring. For example, you can choose to schedule a series of weekly appointments ending on January 1, 2001.

SuperCalendar

You can also maintain a Web-based calendar at the site http://www.super-calendar.com. After registering and logging in, your calendar appears, as shown in Figure 14.4.

FIGURE 14.4 SuperCalendar

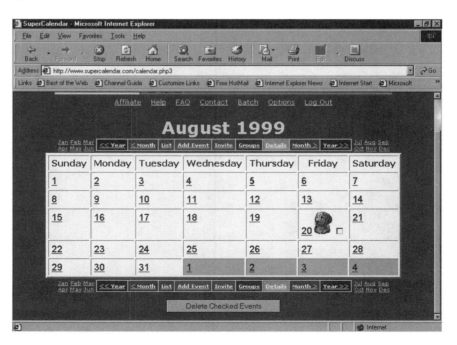

Use the links and options above the calendar to change the month and year, show a list of meetings, and add new ones. You can also invite others to a meeting or join a group.

Some Other PIMS

In addition to the services described in detail above, here are some other Web-based PIMs worth exploring:

NAME	SITE
Day-Timer Digital	http://digital.daytimer.com
Jump	http://www.jump.com
PlanetAll	http://www.planetall.com
MagicalDesk	http://www.magicaldesk.com
When.com	http://www.when.com
Yahoo	http://calendar.yahoo.com

News and Mail

The Internet can keep you informed about current news, weather, and sports. It will also keep you up-to-date on the latest gossip via e-mail from friends and foe alike. Tame the news/mail Internet beast with the features you'll learn here.

15 Where's the Sports Section?

If you're too busy to enjoy reading your local newspaper, or watching the local news over a cup of java in the morning, take a look at the news on-screen.

Read Local News, Weather, and Sports

A growing number of newspapers and television stations are going online with electronic versions of their daily papers and news reports. You can do anything, from reading the current news to checking out the lottery results, and you can generally find out what's happening in your city and around the world—all online.

Here's What You Need

You'll need access to the Internet and a local newspaper or television station that provides online news.

Sites and Features

Probably the best place to start looking for local news, sports, and weather is at `http://dir.yahoo.com/News_and_Media`.

From there, you can choose to view newspapers, magazines, radio stations, television stations, and other types of media. If you select newspapers, for example, you can choose a category of newspaper or select from a list of papers that have online sites.

NOTE Also check out http://www.mediainfo.com/emedia.

The features available once you select a specific paper vary. All of the newspapers let you read the day's top stories and access other sections of the paper. The *Houston Chronicle* has links to various sections of its paper along the left of the screen. The home page of the *Philadelphia Inquirer* is similar, with tabs along the top of the page to go to major sections of the paper, or the links along the left to search by category.

If you select magazines from the Yahoo! site, you can first select a category, as shown in Figure 15.1, and then a specific magazine. Radio and television stations work about the same way.

FIGURE 15.1 Magazine categories

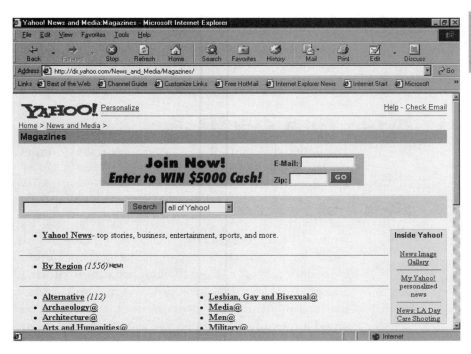

If you're interested in news, local or not, then try `http://www.totalnews.com`. You can search for news stories based on a keyword or you can click a category from a collection of links. Clicking a link shows a list of sources for news—print and broadcast. Pick the source you want to review and then read the news!

16 Appearing at a Location Near You

If you're looking for a good movie to see, a concert to attend, or just what special events are going on in your city, then log on to the Internet.

Locate Local Entertainment

It seems like just about everyone is on the Internet. Chances are your city is too. Through local government, neighborhood organizations, and companies home pages, you can learn what's happening in your city or town.

Here's What You Need

The only things you will need are access to the Internet and the name of the city you want information about.

Sites and Features

Some city listings in the Internet are detailed—with movie locations and times, happenings in local clubs, charity events, and the like. Others are more commercially oriented, with restaurant information, tourist sites, and other standard information. And remember, you can use city information not just for your own town but for places you plan to visit. Be prepared for a rainy night when you're at the beach, or to take advantage of those special events in far away places.

Sidewalk

The best place to start is at the sidewalk—`sidewalk.com`, that is. Try entering this in the address line: `http://yourcity.sidewalk.com/entertainment`.

Of course, substitute *yourcity* with the name of your town, as in `http://sanfransicso.sidewalk.com/entertainment`. If your city is covered by the sidewalk service, you'll see information as shown in Figure 16.1.

FIGURE 16.1 City entertainment information on Sidewalk

If your town has this option, get movie listings by clicking the *Movies* link in the left-hand column. In the screen that appears, pull down the list at the Fast Finder box to see a list of films playing in your town. Click a film title to see a summary of it, and click the link *Show times listed below* to see the locations and times it is playing. With Netscape Navigator, you will need to choose the film from the pull-down list and then click the Go button.

If you get an error message, then your city is not among those maintained in this site's database. In that case, try `http://national.sidewalk.msn.com`, which accesses the service's main home page and displays this dialog box:

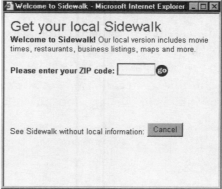
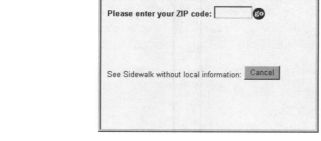

Enter your ZIP code and click Go. You can then click Entertainment Guide in the screen that appears to access listings for movies, concerts, and other activities.

Once you access a city using Sidewalk it places a cookie on your system. When you next go to the national sidewalk site, it gets the city from the cookie and automatically displays that city page. To get information from another city, click the link *select a new city.*

infospace.com

Another way to find information on your town is to navigate to `http://infospace.com` and click the *City Guide* link. In the screen that appears, enter your city and state, or your zip code, and click the Get City button. In addition to other information on your city, you'll see links to access categories of information.

One special feature of Infospace is their community message boards. You can leave and reply to messages, sharing information with friends and strangers, about almost anything. Look under the Regional Message Boards headings on the Infospace screen; there you will see the beginning of a list of message boards. To view more links, click *More....*

You can read messages very easily; just click a topic to see the individual messages, and then click a message that you want to read. If you want to leave a message or reply to one, however, you have to sign up for a free Infospace account. The first time you click either Post a Message or Reply, you'll be asked for your Infospace username and password. If you haven't yet signed up, click the *Sign Up For My Infospace* link, and complete the requested information.

Other Options

When neither Sidewalk nor Infospace contain the local information you're looking for, try working through your state. To access your state's home page, go to `http://www.state.`*`yourstate`*`.us`, as in `http://www.state.ca.us` for California, or `http://www.state.pa.us` for Pennsylvania. Once you get to your state's home page, look for links to local communities.

17 Breaking News, as It Happens

Watch late-breaking news, sports, and weather scroll across your screen, and customize news reports to get just what you are interested in knowing.

View Headline News

You'll get the latest headlines delivered right to your screen, and if you see a story you're interested in, just click to get all of the details.

Here's What You Need

You'll need an Internet provider that offers a dial-up networking connection and a news-broadcasting program that you can find on the CD or download from the Internet.

Sites and Features

Getting news delivered right to your desktop is called *push technology* because information from the Internet is pushed your way—it goes to you rather than you requesting a site to be downloaded. To get information pushed to your screen, you'll need a news service program. The program accesses the service's Web site and downloads the current headlines and news, which it displays on your screen. The programs and the service are free. You "pay" for it by seeing ads for sponsors along with the headlines. It is a small price to pay, however, for being kept informed in real-time. If the ads bother you, there are programs that can keep some of them away, as you'll learn in Section 38, *Busting Those Ads*.

You can specify the type of news you'd like to receive and, in some cases, even customize it for your location. Of course, you'll need to be online to receive the news, but as you're working or browsing, you'll see headlines scroll across your screen. One program even replaces your screen saver, so the news continues even during periods of inactivity.

There are a number of push programs available for free on the Internet. We've included one of them, NewsWatch, on the CD with this book. Let's take a look at NewsWatch first, and then at one of the most popular and powerful programs, PointCast.

NewsWatch

Newscast is provided by DigiBand, the same folks who created EarthTuner for listening to radio broadcasts from around the world. You'll find News-Watch on the CD, or you can download it from http://www.digiband.com.

When you start NewsWatch, it dials into your ISP (if you are not already connected), and starts displaying the current headlines in its own on-screen window. The news is drawn from a list of sites maintained by Digiband.

N O T E Be patient. It may take a few seconds for the news to be retrieved and displayed.

News is retrieved and updated every 45 seconds. A different source is used for each update. The source of the headlines currently displayed is shown on the top line of the NewsWatch window, along with the number of seconds until the next update. To update earlier just click the second display.

To read details of a story, click the headline. You can also click the source to go to its home page. To update the list of sources, click Menu on the News-Watch window and choose Update Site list.

You can customize NewsWatch in several ways. First, if you access the Internet through a proxy server, click Menu and choose Internet Options. In the dialog box that appears, enter the proxy server name. You can also use this dialog box to specify the Web browser you want to use to display news.

To customize the type of news that appears, click Menu and choose Preferences. In the dialog box that appears, you can unsubscribe to categories so they do not appear, and adjust how often headlines scroll and are updated. You can also change the colors used to display headlines.

PointCast

The PointCast program and network is one of the most popular because of the range of services that it offers. You can download the program from http://www.pointcast.com using these steps:

1. Log on to your ISP and go to http://www.pointcast.com.

2. Click the *Download* link on the top of the page. You'll now see a series of screens for choosing the file for downloading.

3. Select the option button for your operating system and then click Next. Your choices are Windows 95, 98, NT 4, or Windows 3.1.

4. Choose the language you want the program in, and then click Next.

5. Choose the location nearest you and then click Next.

6. There are two buttons, one labeled "Download via FTP!" and the second labeled "Download via HTTP!" Try the FTP button first. If that fails, try the HTTP button.

When you first run the program, you'll be asked some registration information, such as your zip code, e-mail address, and your main areas of interest. The information is used to help PointCast determine the type of information to push your way. Because my zip code is near Philadelphia, PA, for example, I get the option of going to the Web site of the *Philadelphia Inquirer*, `http://www.philly.com`, on the PointCast window. If you check off that you are interested in work with computers, you'll get computer news by default. You can also choose to link PointCast to a Web browser that you already have installed, or to the browser built into PointCast.

The PointCast window includes the *ticker*—a bar of scrolling information along the bottom of the screen. The ticker is set to stay on-screen even when you switch to another application so you can view headlines as you work.

Listed down the left-hand side of the screen are channels—categories of information that you can request to be displayed. You can scroll the channels by clicking the arrow buttons above and below the channel list. The exact channels that appear depend on the answers you gave when you first start the program.

Below the channels are buttons to perform PointCast functions. Click Update All to dial into your ISP and retrieve the current news and headlines. Here are some of the other commands:

Personalize   Lets you customize PointCast.

View   Lets you hide or display the ticker and the PointCast Smart Screen that acts as a screen saver.

Print   Lets you print the selected news story.

Help   Shows you how to use PointCast.

Internet   Launches your Web browser and connects to the ISP.

The channel you select may be divided into categories and shown to the right of the channel list. For example, the CNN channel has two categories, News and Features. The tabs let you further choose the type of information. The News category of CNN, for example, contains Top Sites, U.S. News, World News, and Politics News. The Features category offers Sci-Tech, Travel, and Health. Select a category and then area of interest to see the latest headlines below the tabs. Then, click a headline to read about it in the PointCast window.

The upper-right window in PointCast shows advertisements. Most of them will be animated, so you may see a mouse pointer move around or some cute little characters.

Personalizing PointCast   You can customize PointCast to get the type of news that you're interested in. You can only set personalization options when offline, so if you're connected to the PointCast network, click the Stop button. (It replaces Update All when online.)

Next click Personalize for these options: Add/Remove Channels, Personalize Channels, and Application Settings.

Selecting Add/Remove Channels opens the dialog box shown in Figure 17.1. The list on the left shows all of the channels that PointCast makes available. The list on the right shows channels that are being monitored and displayed on your screen.

To add a new channel, click it from the list on the left, and then click the Add button. You are allowed only 12 channels. To remove a channel, click it from the list on the right, and then click the Remove button. Icons next to the channel names on the right indicate their type or status. Mandatory channels, by the way, are required as part of PointCast's advertising agreements.

To personalize channels, click the Personal Channels button in the Add/Remove Channels box, or choose Personalize Channels from the Personalize menu. PointCast opens a dialog box with a tab for each active channel. The options on the tabs vary according to the channel, so review each tab and make any desired changes. For example, the Weather tab lets you select up to 50 cities to track for weather, to show forecasts and weather maps, and to display the temperatures in Celsius or Fahrenheit.

Use the Companies channel to track your stock portfolio and market indicators.

Choosing Application Settings from the Personalize menu opens the dialog box in Figure 17.2.

FIGURE 17.1   **Personalizing PointCast**

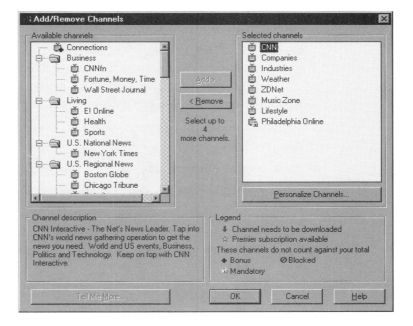

FIGURE 17.2   **PointCast settings**

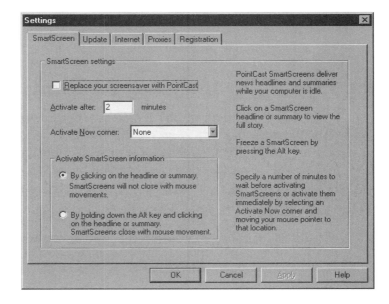

Here is a list of the tabs on this screen and what they are responsible for.

SmartScreen tab   Lets you control how PointCast acts as a screen saver, such as when and how it appears on screen.

Update tab   Controls when headlines and news are updated. You can choose to update continuously (recommended for a direct Internet connection), when you click Update All, or on a schedule. If you choose to update on schedule, you can pick the times and days.

Internet tab   Lets you choose your dial-up connection, browser, and mail settings.

Proxies tab   Allows you to specify a proxy server.

Registration tab   Allows you to change your registration information.

Finally, to customize the ticker, click the button on the ticker's far upper left and choose Personal Ticker from the pop-up menu. In the dialog box that appears you can choose which channels are displayed on the ticker.

18   Free E-Mail

Think that one e-mail account is enough? No way! There are plenty of reasons to sign up for more free e-mail accounts.

Sign Up for Free E-Mail Accounts

Free e-mail offers are all over the Internet, and millions of folks are taking advantage of them. Why do companies offer e-mail for free? Repeat after me—ADVERTISING. The more hits, the more revenue, and the more likely you are to partake in some of the fee-based services that are available.

Here's What You Need

You'll need access to the Internet. You don't even need to have an ISP, you just need to be able to get into the Internet from any location.

Sites and Features

Your first question may be "why do I need more than one e-mail address?" Oh, let me count the ways...

◆ Do you have an e-mail account at work and think (or know) your boss is reading your mail? Sign up for free e-mail to keep your personal mail just that—personal.

◆ Do you share an e-mail account with other members of your family and know that your spouse/children/significant other is reading your mail? Use free e-mail so every member of your family has their own address. (Some ISPs let you sign up for more than one e-mail address on one account anyway.)

◆ Do you have an ISP that you can only access from your home computer, or where their special software is installed? Get free e-mail so you can get your mail from any computer connected to the Internet.

◆ Are you getting too much junk e-mail? Get a free e-mail account to use when filling out forms so junk mail is channeled there.

◆ Would you like an e-mail address with a snappy name, like `computer-author@hotmail.com`? Yep, you can do that with free e-mail.

◆ Want to send an electronic complaint but not under your "real" address? Sign up for a free e-mail address and complain from there.

◆ Would you like to double-up on some free offers? You don't know if the folks who give the offers would appreciate this, but many of them use your e-mail address to check if you've already signed up. With a free e-mail account, you get another address to use.

If you answered YES! to any of those questions, then you are a perfect candidate for free e-mail. Here are some facts about free e-mail accounts.

All of the free e-mail programs are Web based. This means that you don't need any special software to get your e-mail, and you can get it from ANY location that has access to the Internet. You won't need any special e-mail program or special program provided by the ISP. You can get your mail from the library, school, the local Internet café, anywhere there is an Internet connection you can use.

The free e-mail programs are server based. This means that the e-mail is stored on their computer even after you read it. So if you check your mail at work, it will still be there for you to read again when you get home. You have to tell the system to delete it.

Some of the services also provide e-mail forwarding. This means that you can have mail from other accounts sent to their server. So all of your mail will be waiting for you in one location. The one drawback is that many of the services add a small ad to each message you send.

Who offers free e-mail? Just about everyone:

- ◆ http://www.excite.com
- ◆ http://www.homepageware.com
- ◆ http://www.lycos.com
- ◆ http://www.netscape.com
- ◆ http://www.visto.com
- ◆ http://www.yahoo.com
- ◆ http://www.iname.com
- ◆ http://www.mail.com

Hotmail

You almost can't browse anywhere on the Internet without tripping over a free e-mail program.

As an example, let's look at signing up for free mail on http://www.hotmail.com, a very popular free e-mail service. The process is about the same with the others, only the links are different.

1. Log on to http://www.hotmail.com.

2. Click Sign Up Now!

3. Read the legalese in the Terms of Service document that appears, and then scroll to the end and click I Accept.

4. Enter the information requested. This includes entering a login name that will be your e-mail name, a password, your first and last name, your country, gender, and the year of your birth. You can also choose to have your name and location listed in the Hotmail directory and to have Hotmail add your name and e-mail address to general Internet directories.

5. When you're done, click Submit Registration.

You can enter your login name and password to access your Hotmail e-mail and to send e-mail from the initial Hotmail screen.

A typical Hotmail inbox is shown in Figure 18.1. You can read or delete messages, move a message to another folder, and create a new message. The options next to Inbox let you look for new mail that might have been delivered to your Hotmail address or get mail from other mail servers. If you click POP Mail, you can designate up to four mail servers that this e-mail will be linked to, such as your ISP or other free mail systems. Among other features, Hotmail and similar services let you create an online address book. Click Addresses from the list of options across the top to open your address book. Here you can add recipients and give them nicknames.

FIGURE 18.1 Hotmail inbox

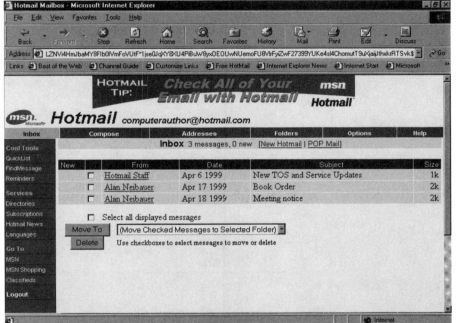

To read a message, click its link. To delete mail, enable the check box next to it and click delete. You can also move an e-mail to one of the other folders that Hotmail provides—Sent Messages, Drafts, the Trash Can, or a custom folder that you create.

To send a message, click Compose along the top of the screen. The mail composition window is shown in Figure 18.2. You can either type the recipient's e-mail address in the To line, or click To to access your address book.

If you click the QuickList button, you also access your nicknames in the main browser window. The same goes for the cc and bcc lines. You can also click QuickList to access a list of recipient nicknames.

Enter the subject of the message and then its text. Using the buttons, you can save the message in your Drafts folder, add an attachment, check your spelling, use the thesaurus, or look up a word in the dictionary. Click Egreetings to select and send an electronic greeting card, as you'll learn how to do in Section 22.

When you're done with the message click Send.

FIGURE 18.2   **Composing mail with Hotmail**

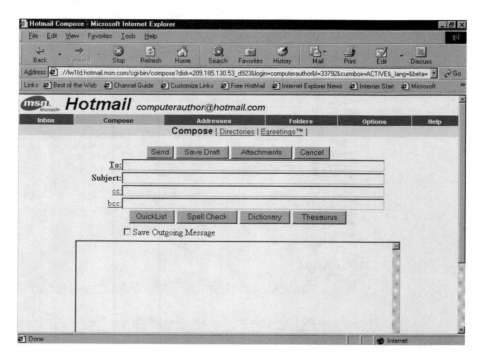

Also, the Stationery Chooser button and Use Stationery list let you decorate your e-mail with a fancy graphic design. Pull down the Use Stationery list, for example, to select from over 20 complete stationery designs.

The Stationery Chooser button opens a dialog box in which you can see a preview of each design before you choose one.

19 Access Multiple E-Mail Accounts

Some Internet providers give you more than one e-mail account. You might use the accounts for each member of the family, or just use different names for various purposes, such as business and personal. But having multiple accounts means you have to remember to check for mail on each. No problem.

Retrieve E-Mail for Multiple Accounts Simultaneously

Once you have more than one e-mail account, you have to remember to check each for new mail. With all of the free mail offers available, and with multiple accounts at one ISP, you could end up checking two, three, four, or more mail accounts each time. It would be too easy to skip an account, and miss some important piece of mail.

Here's What You Need

You'll need a program that lets you access multiple accounts at one time. There is one free with Microsoft Internet Explorer—Outlook Express—and you'll find another on the CD that comes with this book.

Sites and Features

Checking more than one mail account at a time is easy. In fact, you can take advantage of free or inexpensive software to automatically check all of your accounts at the same time.

Using Outlook Express

Outlook Express is an e-mail program that comes free with Microsoft Internet Explorer, which comes free with Microsoft Office and plenty of other programs. With Outlook, you set up one or more accounts that you want to use to send and receive mail. You can choose to send and receive from any or all accounts at the same time.

To set up an account in Outlook Express, start the program and then follow these steps.

1. Select Tools ➤ Accounts to open the Internet Accounts dialog box.

2. Click the Mail tab, then the Add, and choose Mail. This starts the Internet Connection Wizard.

3. Enter the details of your account in the dialog boxes that follow. You will be asked for the name that you want displayed in messages, your e-mail address, the type of server, and the name of the ingoing and outgoing servers, and your account name and password.

4. Click Finish in the last Wizard.

NOTE Outlook Express 5 also lets you sign up for a Hotmail account and send and receive Hotmail mail. To sign up for a Hotmail account, choose Tools ➤ New Account Signup ➤ Hotmail. Follow the steps shown previously for adding a new account, but specify your Hotmail address in the second Wizard dialog box.

When you click Finish in the last wizard dialog box, your accounts will be listed in the Accounts dialog box. The default account will be used automatically for all mail that you send. You can tell which account is the default by looking for the word *(default)* in the list of accounts. Use the Set as Default button to select another account as your default.

Before using the account, follow these steps:

1. Click the account in the Accounts dialog box.

2. Click Properties to see the dialog box in Figure 19.1.

3. In the text box at the top, enter the name that you want to appear for the mail account in Outlook Express boxes.

4. Notice the check box at the bottom labeled Include This Account When Receiving Mail or Synchronizing. Enable the check box if you want Outlook Express to automatically include this account when you send and receive mail.

5. Click the Connection tab.

6. Click Always Connect Using, and then select the dial-up networking account.

7. Click OK.

FIGURE 19.1 **Account properties**

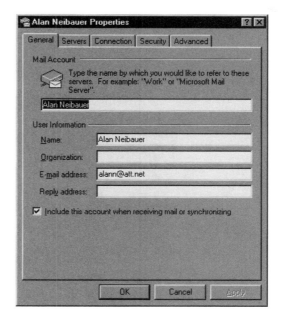

Now when you are ready to send mail, you have to select the account to use. Click New Mail in the Outlook Express toolbar to open a mail window. Pull down the list at the end of the From box and select the mail account that you want to use. Complete the message and then click Send.

NOTE The instructions for sending mail are for Outlook Express version 5. If you have an earlier version of the program, complete the mail messages, choose File ➤Send Later Using, and then click the account to use.

When you click Send, Outlook Express adds the message to your Outbox. If Outlook Express isn't set up to send your mail immediately, click the Send/Rec button on the toolbar. Outlook Express dials your Internet provider, sends your mail from your Outbox, and checks for new mail. If you want to send mail without checking for new messages, pull down the list next to the Send/Rec button and choose Send All. You can also choose a specific account to use.

Changing Identities When you check for mail with multiple accounts set up, all new mail appears in the same inbox. So, you'll be able to read everyone's mail, and they'll be able to read yours. If you want to keep your mail separate and private, create an *identity* for each member of the family who has an e-mail account. The identity records the person's name and e-mail address, and creates an entirely new set of folders for each.

To create an identity, choose File ➢ Identities ➢ Add New Identity to open the dialog box shown here:

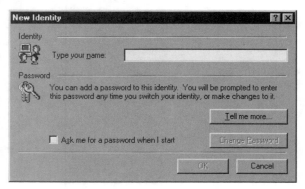

Type a name for the identity. If you want to password protect the folders so others cannot read the identity's e-mail, click Ask Me For a Password When I Start. Enter the password in both text boxes and click OK.

Now click OK in the New Identity dialog box. You'll be asked if you want to switch to that identity. If you select Yes, a whole new set of Outlook Express folders appears. If you select No, you can later change identities by selecting File ➢ Switch Identity. This will open the box shown in Figure 19.2. Click the identity in the box that appears, and then click OK.

FIGURE 19.2 Switching identities

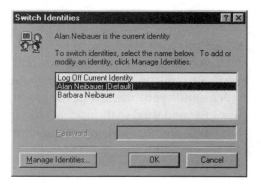

For each identity, you have to create an e-mail account. So when you first create the identity, the Internet Connection Wizard starts. You'll first be asked if you want to use an existing account or create a new one. Click Create a New Internet Mail Account and then click Next. Complete the Wizard and then click Finish.

To choose which identity to use as the default when you start Outlook Express, select File ➤ Identities ➤ Manage Identities to see a list of defined identities. Choose the identity to use as the default, and then click the Make Default button. Select Ask Me in this list if you want to choose the identity when you start Outlook Express.

Before creating or sending mail, make sure you are using your own identity. Choose File ➤ Switch Identity; click the identity in the box that appears, and then click OK.

NOTE The Netscape Navigator Web browser supports "profiles" that are totally separate environments for each user. Each user specifies their own e-mail configurations, and they get their own browser bookmarks and other settings. You get to choose a profile when you start up Netscape, if you have more than one.

Using Ristra Mail Monitor

Free mail services such as Hotmail, Netscape, and Excite are called *HTTP mail systems* because you send and receive mail directly from the Internet—at their HTTP Web site.

If you have several of these free mail accounts, you can check them all for new mail using a program called Ristra Mail Monitor. You'll find an evaluation copy of the program on the accompanying CD or you can download it from `http://www.download.com`.

Running the program places an icon for it in the system tray on the Windows taskbar. It also adds it to the Start group so the program runs automatically each time you start Windows. Right-click the icon to display these options:

View Status
Check Mail Now
Open Settings...
Disable Mail Check
Help Topics
Registration
About Mail Monitor
Exit

You have to first set up the program to access each of your Web-based e-mail accounts. To do this, follow these steps.

1. Select Open Settings from the shortcut menu to open the Ristra Mail Monitor Setting dialog box.

2. Click Add to see a list of accounts.

3. Enter your login name and the name of the service to complete your e-mail address. You can also pull down the list at the end of the Login Name box to select from supported services.

4. Next, enter your password and click Confirm. The e-mail address will be added to the List of Mail Accounts box.

5. Click the Preference tab.

6. Enable the check box labeled Automatically Enter Login and Password When Logging In to the Mail Account. This setting will check for mail without you having to enter the login information to have Ristra check the mail.

When you want to check your mail at all of the accounts, just click Check Mail in the Settings dialog box, or choose Check Mail Now from the Ristra shortcut menu on the system tray. Ristra dials into your ISP and checks for new mail at each of the listed services, displaying the results in the Status dialog box.

To read mail, click the account and then click Log In to read your mail.

Other programs for checking multiple mail accounts include Cyber-Info Webmail Notify from `http://www.cyber-info.com` and @nymail from `http://www.tntsb.com/anymail`.

20 Eating Spam

Spam is a meat-based product manufactured by Hormel Foods Corporation. But the Internet community has further immortalized Spam so that it has come to mean unsolicited e-mails that are sent to a large number of users on the Internet. No matter how you feel about the meat-based product (try it grilled like a hamburger…), the Internet type of Spam is bad.

Stop Junk Mail

If you're getting tired of the junk mail that fills up your inbox, strike back. You can prevent junk mail from ever reaching your computer.

Here's What You Need

You'll need an e-mail program with a junk mail filter, or one of the programs you can find on the CD with this book – Spam Eater and SpamOff.

Sites and Features

An occasional piece of spam wouldn't be too bad, but have you been hit by five, ten, or more chunks of spam at the same time? If not, you probably will be. Here's the typical scenario—you see that 20 e-mails are coming in, get excited because you think you're so popular, and then you find out it's the same spammer flooding your inbox.

Fighting Back

Fighting back is not always easy, but there are steps you can take. First, you can try contacting your ISP to see if they can take some action by blocking known spammers. Many ISPs offer customer support advice for dealing with junk mail.

You can also try responding to the spam by asking to be removed from the list. Some spammers even tell you how to be removed from their list by returning the message with Remove as the subject, or by e-mailing another address. This doesn't work all of the time though. Some spammers send out their junk and close down the address so your reply is returned; some spammers welcome your reply because it confirms that your e-mail address is legitimate, and therefore they will continue to send you junk mail.

You could also try flooding the spammer's mailbox with your own junk mail and long file attachments, a technique called *bombing*. But this doesn't work and most of the time all of your junk mail to them will bounce right back.

You can also send an e-mail to the spammer's domain. If you get junk mail from someone at America Online, for example, send a complaint to `abuse@aol.com`. With other ISPs try `postmaster@their_domain_name`.

The fight against junk mail is far from hopeless, especially with a little help from the Internet and software developers.

Some e-mail programs, for example, maintain junk mailer lists. E-mail addresses that you add to the list can be deleted as soon as they come in. You don't actually avoid downloading their messages, you just don't see them.

In Microsoft's Outlook Express, for example, select a junk mail message in the Inbox, and then choose Block Sender from the Message menu. You'll see a message asking if you want to also delete all of the messages from that sender. Click Yes if you do. When any new mail arrives from the sender, it will automatically be moved to the Deleted Items folder.

If you change your mind about blocking mail from the sender, select Message Rules from the Tools menu and click Blocked Senders List. In the dialog box that appears, select the e-mail address of the person you no longer want to block and click Remove. Select Yes to confirm the deletion, and then close the Message Rules dialog box.

SpamEater and Spam Off

An even better solution to junk messages, however, is to delete them even before they download into your computer. If you get your mail over the Internet through a POP3 mail server, you can do just that. There are programs that dial into your ISP's post office and check the mail waiting for you. If the program finds an address or domain that you've identified as junk, it deletes the message without having to download it. You'll find two such programs on the CD with this book.

 SpamEater comes with a long list of known spammers, but you can add your own as well. There is a standard version that is distributed for free and a professional version with additional features available for a 30-day trial period. The trial version is on the CD with this book. You can download the freeware version from http://www.zdnet.co.uk/software/free/internet/email/sw32.html.

The program can automatically check for spam and delete it, or it will let you view your messages' headers (the To, From, and Subject part of the message) to determine which you want to delete.

To see how SpamEater operates, choose Preferences from the File menu to create a profile in the dialog box shown in Figure 20.1. You will see that the profile includes the address of your ISP's e-mail server and your logon name and password. You use the Spammers tab of the dialog box to view the list of known spammers, and to add your own.

FIGURE 20.1 SpamEater

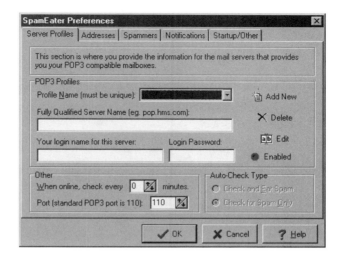

You then use the Action menu in the SpamEater window to perform these actions:

Check and Eat Spam　Checks your waiting mail and deletes messages from people on the spammers list.

Check Only for Spam　Scans your mailbox for spam.

Check and View Headers　Displays the headers of messages so you can delete interactively.

 Spam Off is another anti-spam program that you'll find on the CD or download from `http://www.shareit.com` or `http://www.1elsoft.hypermart.net/spamoff`. It works about the same way SpamEater does, deleting messages from identified spammers. After installing the program, right-click its icon in the system tray, as shown here:

Use the Mail Options menu choice to specify your e-mail server, login name, and password.

Use the Kill List command to designate the e-mail addresses of spammers or just their domains. The capability of adding domains to the list, rather than specific addresses on the domain, lets you capture spam from anyone using a spam-friendly mail server.

Select Check Mail Now to dial into your e-mail server and delete messages from listed spammers.

For more information and programs about fighting spam, check out these sites:

◆ http://www.junkbusters.com/ht/en/index.html

◆ http://www.mindworkshop.com/alchemy/nospam.html

◆ http://www.cyber-info.com

◆ http://www.spamkiller.com

More Free Stuff

So far, you've learned how to get free music, videos, and e-mail over the Internet, but that just touches on the free stuff that's available. There are all sorts of free things that you can get, so put your charge card away!

21 Test Free Service Offers

Whoever said "there's no such thing as a free lunch" was never the lucky recipient of those free America Online (AOL) CDs clogging up the mailbox. Don't throw them away! Even if you already have an ISP, you should take advantage of the free trial offers provided by AOL and other companies.

Enjoy Free Internet Access

The free monthly offers from ISPs (such as AOL, CompuServe, and others) let you browse the Internet, send and receive e-mail, and download files at no risk. The offers are especially attractive if your current ISP charges for extra hours or does not have a local toll-free number. After all, the trial period is free, and you just might find an ISP you like better!

Here's What You Need

You'll need a credit card and a calendar. And sometimes the patience to wait on hold for a long time!

Sites and Features

Suppose you want to download some humongous file, or you need to spend an extended period online browsing. If you have limited free time on your ISP, you'll find it gets used up quickly.

Rather than waste your precious money, take advantage of free monthly offers. Sign up, download those large files, or do that extended browsing, and then cancel the service. The trick is to cancel the service BEFORE the free time period or free hours are exceeded.

First, find out exactly what the free offer entails by asking the following questions:

- ◆ Is it a free month?
  - ◆ Calendar month or 30 days from signing up?
  - ◆ Exactly what is the last free day to use it?
- ◆ Is it free hours?
  - ◆ How many?
  - ◆ When do they start?
  - ◆ When do they end?
  - ◆ What's the charge for additional hours?

Next, be prepared by getting any required software first. If you didn't get any free CDs in the mail, look for free signup CDs in local computer stores, or packed in computer magazines. When you install the software, choose to retain your current browser if that is an option. This will create less possible havoc if you decide to cancel the ISP after the trial period and remove its software.

Dial-Up Networking

Depending on the service, you may not need any new software. Some ISPs let you connect using the Dial-Up Networking that is built into Windows. You can use whatever browser and e-mail program you already have. So, if you are connected to one ISP through Dial-Up Networking, you might only need to create another connection in the Dial-Up Networking window. This saves you the trouble of installing special software only to uninstall it after the free trial. Some uninstall programs leave too many traces of their programs around anyway.

To find out if you can use Dial-Up Networking rather than the ISP's software, make sure to call the ISP whose trial period you want to use, rather than signing up automatically using their free software. If they will let you sign up without using their software, ask them to provide you with the local telephone number to dial, your user name, and your password.

Also ask them to give you the Dial-Up Networking type (usually PPP: Internet, Windows NT Server, Windows 98), the primary DNS, the secondary DNS, and any other Dial-Up Networking (DUN) settings.

Once you've given them your charge card information, follow these steps:

1. Open My Computer and then Dial-Up Networking.

2. Open Make New Connection to see the first Make New Connection dialog box, shown in Figure 21.1.

FIGURE 21.1   **Making a new connection**

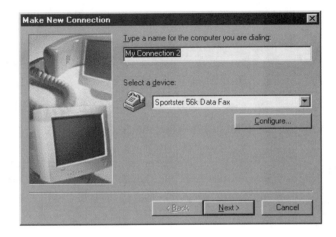

3. Type a name for the connection.

4. If the modem listed is incorrect, pull down the list under the Select a Device heading, and choose the modem you want to use. Click the Configure button only if you need to change any of the modem settings, AND YOU REALLY KNOW WHAT YOU ARE DOING.

5. Click Next to see the second Make New Connection dialog box.

6. Enter the area code and phone number of the free-trial ISP.

7. Click Next to see the last Make New Connection dialog box.

8. Click Finish.

9. Now right-click the connection you just made (it will have the name you entered in step 3 above) and choose Properties. The first tab of the box that appears should show the same phone number and modem you setup in the Make New Connection boxes. If not, enter the correct number and choose the correct modem.

10. Now click the Server Types tab to see the options shown in Figure 21.2.

FIGURE 21.2 Setting dialup properties

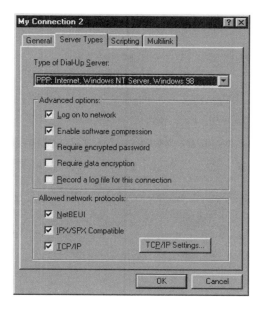

11. Check the setting in the Type of Dial-Up Server box. It should normally be PPP: Internet, Windows NT Server, Windows 98.

12. Make sure the Advanced Options are set correctly. If you are unsure, leave them alone.

13. Click the TCP/IP Settings button.

14. If your ISP gave you a DNS number, enable the option Specify Name Server Address.

15. Enter the Primary DNS.

16. Enter the Secondary DNS, if you were given one by the ISP.

17. Click OK until all of the dialog boxes are closed.

You now have more than one Dial-Up Networking connection created. To dial into the trial ISP, double-click the connection you created for it. The first time you connect, you'll have to enter your user name and password.

Enter the information, and enable the option labeled Save Password. Once the connection is made, start your browser—you're ready to go!

Some ISPs let you bring your own Internet connection. This means that you can save money if you sign up for two Internet services by using one to connect to the other. You'll learn more about this later. Do not select this option for your trial period. Why? With BYO, you dial into the new ISP through your current one, so you are still using its dial-up network and accumulating usage time.

Additional Information

Try these Web sites to check out information about free trial periods: http://www.worldnet.att.net, http://www.aol.com, http://www.compuserve.com, and http://www.prodigy.com.

Now about canceling. Make sure you can cancel using a toll-free phone number. Being able to cancel online is fine, but the time spent canceling could bring you over the allowed limit. If you can cancel by phone, this is where the patience referred to earlier comes in. Sometimes, and depending on when you call, the wait to speak with a service representative can be interminable.

Software for signing up with the Earthlink service (a leading ISP) is included with accompanying CD.

22 Don't Lick Stamps!

While not everyone is online, a heck of a lot of people are. So for birthdays, anniversaries, and other occasions, consider sending your greeting card electronically. Your friends and relatives will love getting animated and musical greetings, with personalized messages, delivered directly to their computer screen.

Send E-Cards for Every Occasion

Most online cards are FREE, and most include snappy animations and music. You select the type of card, what you want it to look like, and add your own custom text. There are cards for birthdays, anniversaries, and almost every other imaginable holiday. There are even cards for breaking up a relationship.

Here's What You Need

All you need to send electronic greeting cards is access to the Internet!

Sites and Features

Electronic greeting cards are quick and easy to send. The cards work in two ways.

1. With most systems, the recipient gets an e-mail informing them that an online greeting is waiting for them. All they do is click a link in the e-mail to launch their Web browser and get the card on their screen. Cards are saved from one to three weeks, depending on the company.

2. Other companies let you download the card to your computer, or purchase it on a CD, where you customize it and send it as an e-mail attachment. The recipient just opens the attachment to view the card without having to stay online.

N O T E If you want to send real greeting cards through the mail for a fee, check out `http://www.sparks.com`.

Free and Low-Cost Electronic Greeting Cards

There are hundreds of sites that provide free or low cost cards, but the ones I like best are `http://www.egreetings.com`, `http://www.bluemountain.com`, and `http://www.barkingcard.com`. These sites have plenty of choices, and they provide special holiday cards for almost every occasion.

Egreetings The first time you send a card, you have to register by giving your e-mail address and picking a password. Registration is free. Then, whenever you want to send another card, just sign in with your e-mail address and password. For example, here's how to use E-greetings.

1. Navigate to `http://www.egreetings.com`.

2. Click one of the featured categories in the center of the page. You'll now see several choices of cards.

3. Click the link under the graphic for the card that you want to send. If you click the graphic itself, you'll see how it looks full size.

4. Now fill out the card, enter the recipient's e-mail address, and then fill in a subject line and any personal text you want to enter.

5. Click Preview to see how your card looks or click Send to send it immediately.

6. If you selected to preview the card, click Send to send the card, or Change if you want to modify it.

The recipient gets an e-mail message that includes a link that the recipient can click to go directly to the card at the Egreetings site to see the card.

Blue Mountain Arts The Blue Mountain Arts site works about the same way, and also has a wide variety of cards to select.

1. Navigate to http://www.bluemountain.com, and select the category and the card.

2. When the sample card appears, click the link that says *Personalize and Send*. You'll now see a screen that lets you customize the card by entering the name and e-mail address of the recipient, your own e-mail address and name, and one or more lines of a custom message.

3. Complete all of the information and then click Preview Here Before Sending.

4. If the card looks OK, click Send. Otherwise, you can click Edit Before Sending to make any necessary changes. For some cards, you may even be able to select the date you wish to send it.

You will get an e-mail confirming that the card has been sent, and the recipient gets an e-mail message telling them that you've sent them an electronic card. The recipient should click the link to go directly to the Blue Mountain Arts site to see the card.

Barking Cards Barking Cards, at http://www.barkingcard.com, is a FEE-BASED greeting card company. Barking Cards offers a free sample collection of cards, which are included on the accompanying CD or are available for download from http://www.barkingcard.com. Run the Setup program to install the sample value pack on your computer. If you order an e-mail card online (usually less than $2 a card), you fill out some charge card information and enter the name and e-mail address of the recipients.

For a special value, you can purchase value packs of greeting cards on CD-ROM. Each pack includes a number of cards that you can customize with text, graphics, and sounds. You can send these cards to as many people as you want, for as long as you want. You create the card on your computer by first selecting a category and then a specific card. You then modify the card by adding your own text, graphics, and sounds.

When you're done customizing the card, you are asked if you want to save it with the Barking Card Player. The player allows the recipient to install the card on their computer where they can play it. Saving the card without the player lets you later open and edit the card. You must choose to save it with the player before sending it to the recipient.

You send the card as an attachment to an e-mail message. The attachment appears as an executable program that the recipient saves and then runs. Running the program displays the card and adds it as a program item in the recipient's Start ➤ Programs menu so they can view it again and again.

WARNING Because of the chance of a computer virus, be careful when running any executable file that you get over the Internet. Make sure the card is from a reputable and recognized sender. If you do not recognize the name or e-mail address of the sender, or if none are given, do not run the executable program.

More Electronic Card Options

Here's a list of other sites for free or inexpensive electronic cards:

- ◆ http://findmyhome.com/card2.htm
- ◆ http://www.arkworld.com/pete/greetings
- ◆ http://www.123greetings.com
- ◆ http://www.greeting-cards.com/pg/p
- ◆ http://www.hallmarkconnections.com
- ◆ http://www.virtualpresents.com/cards.html

And for that very special occasion, try visiting http://www.c-ya.com. This site specializes in relationship closure cards—when flowers and candy definitely send the wrong message. Just don't mess up and send one of these cards to your current gal or guy.

23 Enjoy Free Faxing

Even though many modems today can send and receive faxes, you're still responsible for the long distance call charges. Rather than make those long distance calls, send faxes free over the Internet!

Fax Documents Anywhere

My wife just hates making long distance fax calls. It's not the money, it's struggling with all of the numbers. She just hopes that she gets the number correct and actually reaches a fax machine. (OK, so maybe the money does enter into it somewhere.)

Faxing is a great way to communicate, but those long distance telephone charges can be a killer. That's assuming you have a fax machine or a fax-modem. Have you ever checked out the prices that some places charge you to fax? It can be up to $4.00 or $5.00 per page. Pretty expensive for the cost of a phone call!

Well, thanks to the kindness of strangers, you can send free faxes from your computer (even without a fax modem) to telephones around the world.

First, there are some caveats:

◆ The totally free fax services are limited to certain geographic areas. They often rely on volunteers to actually make the local connection, and the service is limited to their areas.

◆ The not-so-totally free services let you send a few faxes for free as a way to test their system. Even if you do have to pay, however, it is still sometimes cheaper than the long distance calls.

N O T E   See Section 24, *Free Faxing Revisited,* to find out how you can get a free phone number for receiving faxes!

Here's What You Need

Basically, to take advantage of these services, you won't need anything except your browser and ISP.

Well, you will have to sign up for the free trial service, and some sites do require you to download their software, but this material is free for the trial period. If you use a free fax service, there are programs that help you use it that are also free. Free. Don't you just love that word?

Sites and Features

There are a number of places on the Internet you can go to fax, but let's start with the totally free one—http://www.fax4free.com.

Fax4Free.com

Signing up for the service with Fax4Free.com is free, as is every fax you send to anyplace in the United States. The only drawback, and this can be a big one, is advertising. Each page of every fax you send through the service is covered with advertising from Fax4Free.com and other sponsors of the service. If you only need to send an occasional personal fax, then it pays to use this service. If you need to send faxes to business associates, then you might find the advertising inappropriate.

Free Trial Faxing

Now don't give up hope and spend that money for a phone call if you don't like the advertisements in Fax4Free.com. You can get up to 30 minutes of free faxing from Faxaway (http://www.faxaway.com). With this company, you can send one fax totally free. When you are ready to send your free fax, navigate to the site, click New Users, and then click the link *give Faxaway a try*.

Click the *Here* link to open your e-mail window. The recipient line will read INSERT FAX NUMBER HERE@faxaway.com. Replace INSERT FAX NUMBER HERE with the complete number, including the country code and area code. Complete the subject line, type the body of the fax in the message area, and then send the message.

For additional free faxes (up to 30 minutes of faxing time), you have to sign up; you have to provide both your e-mail address and your credit card information. Faxaway does not charge by the number of pages being faxed, instead, they charge by the time it takes to send the fax.

You cannot send e-mail attachments with the free trial fax, only after registering. For more robust faxing with formatted documents and attachments, you can purchase Faxaway software or download the free version of Fax-omatic Lite from the site. These programs let you fax from any Windows application, such as Microsoft Word.

The site http://www.faxfree.simplenet.com offers a $5.00 gift voucher. You can send one free fax from their page, then, when you register, they will send an e-mail with $5.00 credit (minus the cost of that first fax you sent).

Pay-Per-Fax

If you find that you really like faxing from your computer through the Internet, you can sign up with one of the fee-based services. There are plenty of them.

In addition to Faxaway, you can register for a fax service though `http://www.netscape.com`. An outfit named Qwest runs Netscape's Fax Center. They charge 15 cents per page, with a $2.95 minimum monthly charge, which covers your first 19 pages faxed anywhere in the United States or Canada, but only for each month that you use the service. (International rates vary.) This means that if you do not send a fax during a month, you won't be billed for the $2.95.

Other fax services include

- `http://ourworld.compuserve.com/homepages/pormesan/global/number/bar/distribution.htm`
- `http://arawak.snfc21.pbi.net/rediska/storm/base/make.htm`
- `http://info.ox.ac.uk/fax/`
- `http://www.awa.com/faxinet/faxinet.html`

When you use any of these services, check the directions very carefully. One thing to check with a potential service is how they handle busy signals and uncompleted faxes. Some charge for each attempt to send the fax, even if the fax does not go through. My free fax using Faxaway did not go through because the number was busy, but it still counted as my one free fax.

24 Free Faxing Revisited

If you think you're spending too much for telephone service, then here's your chance to get even with a free fax telephone number. Anyone can send you a fax at that number, just as if they were calling your phone at home.

Get a Free Fax Line

Now this is something that amazes me. You can sign up for a FREE phone number for receiving faxes. The service receives the fax, and then e-mails it to you. That's right—the phone number is all yours.

Here's What You Need

In addition to your e-mail address, you have to agree to complete a periodic survey or questionnaire. That's it.

Sites and Features

If you already have a fax machine, or fax modem at home, then why would you need this service? Have you ever been woken up in the middle of the night by some incoming fax? Do you have to remember to turn on your fax machine or get your computer started to receive a fax?

With a free incoming fax service, you don't have to worry about all that. Your own private phone number is ready 24 hours a day, seven days a week to receive incoming faxes. When you're asked for your fax number when filling out a form or by some annoying salesperson, just give them your free one.

How can these companies supply this service for nothing? Surprise, surprise—the sites are advertising-sponsored. Your only obligation is to respond to a periodic e-mailed questionnaire and let the company share the information with its sponsors.

All of this is relatively painless—except for the person sending you the fax, perhaps. You see, the numbers assigned are not necessarily in your local area, so the sender may be charged for long-distance charges.

Receiving Services

We'll take a look at two such services: eFax.com and CallWave. Both services give you a free number for receiving faxes. You can sign up for one or both, and it won't cost you a dime.

eFax.com   If you're not particular about where the fax number is located, you can sign up for a free fax number at `http://www.efax.com`.

Once you complete an online form that asks for your name, e-mail address, zip code, and some other information, you'll be given your private fax number, and then you will receive your PIN number via e-mail. The fax number assigned depends on what they have available at the time. (For instance, the one I received is in Massachusetts even though I live in New Jersey.)

To access your account using your PIN number, follow these steps:

1. Go to `http://www.efax.com`.

2. Click the My Account button. You'll be asked if you want to log on using a secure server. This is the preferred option since you'll be sending your PIN over the Internet. A secure server encrypts the information travelling between browser and server—so anyone snooping will not be able to understand the data.

3. Click Secure Server.

4. In the text boxes that appear, enter your eFax number and PIN.

5. Click Login. You'll see your user profile with your name and address. You'll also have options to change your PIN and specify a password to encrypt the faxes before they are transmitted to you.

6. Click Activity Log. You'll see a list of faxes that have been received and forwarded to you.

7. Click Logout when you're done.

When someone sends a fax to your number, eFax.com converts it into a graphic and e-mails it to you as an attachment readable by Kodak Imaging (this product comes free with Windows 98). You can also use a free program that will be sent to you by eFax.com attached to an e-mail. Once you install the viewing program, double-click the fax attachment in the e-mail message to display it in the viewer.

CallWave   If you want to tell folks you have a West Coast office no matter where you are really located, you can get a fax number in northern California (in the 209, 530, 559, or 916 area codes) by navigating to `http://www.callwave.com/yourportal.html`.

Navigate to the site, complete the application, and you are on your way. Just warn friends and relatives that northern California may be a toll call, unless they are lucky enough to live in that beautiful part of the world. The faxes, like those from eFax.com, arrive as e-mail attachments in a format readable by Kodak Imaging.

Both eFax.com and CallWave offer additional services for a fee, and both reserve the right to discontinue the free number at anytime. However, as of this writing, they do not ask for any charge card information and provide the service for free. Check out `http://www.jfax.com`, an alternative to the services described here.

25 Finding Free Software

In this book's introduction, you learned how to download the programs mentioned in the text. The software mentioned here, however, is just a drop in the bucket, a needle in a haystack, a grain of sand on the beach (you get the point) of the software that's available on the Internet.

Download All Kinds of Free Software

There are literally thousands and thousands of programs out there for the taking. Some are excellent, some are average, and some just outright stink. You should not, however, judge a program by the way it is distributed. Many freeware programs are excellent—they do exactly what they are supposed to do, without bugs.

Here's What You Need

You will, surprisingly enough, need access to the Internet. You should also have an unzipping program, such as WinZip, which you'll find on the accompanying CD.

Sites and Features

What kind of software can you get over the Internet? Almost anything:

Utilities	Browsers	Screen Savers
Sample documents	Graphics	Educational programs
Games	Music and sound	Business programs
Device drivers	Web site tools	Operating systems

There are three general places where you can get software—collections, company home pages, and personal pages.

Collections   Are services that catalog a number of programs. They usually offer a way to search for programs, tell you something about software, and let you download them. Most collections also rate programs; this way you know which are the most popular and dependable.

Home pages   Are the sites maintained by the company that wrote or distributed the program. You can find these by searching the Internet, or by following links from many of the collections.

Personal pages   Are maintained by plain ordinary people like you and me. Often, these sites have the owner's favorite programs and offer them to anyone who is interested.

As a general rule-of-thumb, only download programs from recognized collections and company home pages. Why? Unfortunately, there are some crazies out there. Some people just get their kicks by giving other people misery, and they spread programs with viruses. When you download anything onto your machine, think of it as giving control of your computer to whoever wrote the program.

The vast majority of software collections routinely test their offerings for viruses, so you can be relatively sure they are clean. Companies will also test their software. Let's face it, they are letting you download hoping you'll buy the product, so they want to make a good impression. But if you're surfing the Internet and you run across John Doe's Groovy Web site, you have no idea what you're going to run into.

With the necessary cautions aside, feel free to look for and download software. You can start with your ISP. Most ISPs offer links to software on their home page. Services such as AOL and CompuServe excel in the number of software products they offer and make their software easy to find. But the best collections of software can be found at the sites discussed below. These sites all offer a wide variety of programs. They are easily searchable and grouped by category. Also look for software at Stroud's Consummate Winsock Apps List (http://cws.internet.com/home.html) and SoftSeek (http://www.softseek.com).

NONAGS

NONAGS gets its name by not nagging you on-screen with advertisements; it also specializes in software that follows a similar practice. It offers two types of services—Free and Paid.

Nonpaying members get access to a tremendous range of software. Paying members get access to many more bonuses: special downloads, and free e-mail with five addresses for a one-time, lifetime, membership of $29.95.

NOTE On the NONAGS Web site, you can purchase a set of CDs containing most of the programs available on NONAGS.

When you navigate, you go through a series of steps to start getting files.

1. Navigate to http://www.nonags.com.

2. Click the Software Free Access icon to display a map of the world.

3. Click your part of the world to see a list of mirrors, sites that contain the entire NONAGS collection. A portion of this list is shown in Figure 25.1.

FIGURE 25.1 Nonag file locations

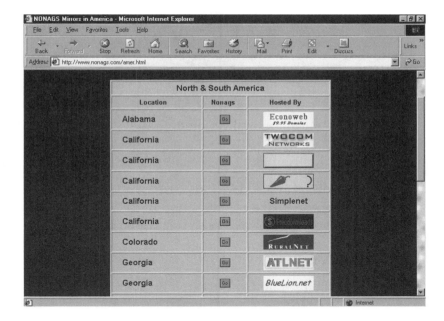

4. Click the GO graphic for the site that is closest to you to open the NONAGS home page.

The What's New section lists recently added or update programs. The category in which the program is located is shown as a colored link.

Click the link to display programs in that category. You can also click any of the links on the left of the screen to navigate through NONAGS, or you can click the *Search* link to enter a search word or phrase for the program you want. The search shows a list of areas in which programs matching your search phrase can be found.

Click one of the links to list the specific files within it. The name of the program is shown first, followed by the date the program was last updated, a link to the company's home page, the name of the author, and a brief description. Below that is an icon representing the NONAGS rating.

To download a program, click its name (the one that appears above the date) to see a dialog box asking if you want to save the program. The dialog box that appears with Microsoft Internet Explorer is shown here:

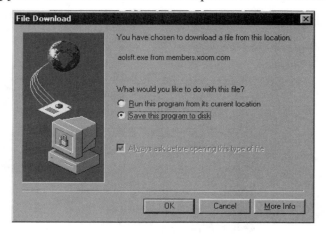

Select Save This Program to Disk, and then click OK. The Save As dialog box appears with a suggested filename. Make sure you record the location where the file will be saved, and then click Save.

winfiles.com

When you navigate to `http://www.winfiles.com`, a site that helps you find freeware or shareware products, click the Search icon in what appears to be a Windows 95/98 window. Enter a word or phrase that describes the type of program you are looking for (such as *graphics* or *virus)*, or enter the name of the program if you know it, and then click Search. You'll see a list of categories that contain files that match your search.

Click a category to display a list of programs. To the right of the program name is a description, the version number, the date and size of the file, the operating system it runs under, and any shareware registration fee. You'll also see any expiration date, if it is a limited time version, and whether it includes installation and removal routines. Below that are approximate download times. Under the description are links you can click to send an e-mail to the program's author or go to the author's home page.

Click the name of the program to start downloading, or click the home page link if you want to read more about the program and download it from the source.

download.com

This site is run by a company called CNET. When you navigate to `http://www.download.com`, click one of the categories that interests you. You may then have to select from a subcategory to see an individual program listing.

You'll see the name of the program, a brief description, the operating system, and its type of license. Click the program name to see more information about the program, and then click Download Now to get your copy of the program.

tucows.com

This sites, pronounced Two-cows, offers a wide range of software organized by operating system. In the main window, `http://www.tucows.com`, you can quickly find a program by typing its name, selecting the operating system, and clicking Search. You will also be asked to select the operating system, and then your region; you can then pick the mirror site that is nearest to you. When your search is complete and you select the program in which you are interested, you'll see the name of the program, followed by its version number and revision date, its file name and size, the type of license, and the cost. You'll also see a link to the author's home page, any other operating systems it is available for, and a description.

Below the description is the Tucows rating, from three cows (OK) to five (excellent). Moo!

26 Get Free Books Online

When you're looking for a classic or something interesting to read, start by looking for it on the Internet. You can download free electronic copies of hundreds of books fairly easily.

Download the Classics and More from the Web

You can actually purchase books, the non-electronic ones with real pages, from a lot of Web sites, as you'll learn in Section 45. But copyrights don't last forever, so many of the old classics can be freely distributed. Since printing, binding, and distributing costs money, you won't find free copies of books unless you're on the Internet.

Here's What You Need

You will need your Web browser, a connection to the Internet, and the sites listed in this chapter.

Sites and Features

You can download the complete versions of many of the best classic books (of course, you will also be able to find some that are not so classic but interesting anyway) directly into your computer. You can then read the book on-screen or print a copy of it to take with you.

Now reading a book on your screen is not as convenient and comfortable as curling up on the sofa with a good book. Reading a long book can be tiring and cause eyestrain. But, on the positive side, you can search the full text of the book to look for names, words, or topics that interest you. If you're a Sherlock Holmes fan, for example, you can search through all of the Sherlock Holmes stories for references to "bullet" to find out where Watson was really wounded. You can also search several versions of the Bible for references and citations.

Project Gutenberg

The best place to start looking for free books is at Project Gutenberg, `http://www.gutenberg.net`. This site has one of the world's largest collections of free books. In addition to Doyle and Shakespeare, you'll find Chekov, Balzac, Butler, Plato, Socrates, Ibanez, Barrie, Milton and thousands of others. It has all six volumes of the *Decline and Fall of the Roman Empire*, the *Warlords of Mars* by Edgar Rice Burroughs, the Bible, the Book of Mormon, *Roget's Thesaurus*, *Aesop's Fables*, and the *CIA World Factbook*.

You'll also find historical documents, such as Lincoln's and Kennedy's inaugural addresses, the Gettysburg Address, the Mayflower Compact, Patrick Henry's Give Me Liberty Or Give Me Death speech, the United States Constitution, the Bill of Rights, and the Declaration of Independence.

Use the links along the left of the Project Gutenberg home page to either search for a book, browse through the Etext listings, or see the most recent editions. You can also download a text or ZIP file containing the complete list of available books.

If you choose Search on the home page, you can search by author, title, subject, or keywords, and you can specify a language and Library of Congress classification. After entering sufficient information to locate the book, click Submit Query.

If you'd rather browse, click Etext Listings on the home page to see two options: Browse Our Etext Listings and Pick an FTP Site.

Selecting the browse option lets you see a list of books by either author or title. Choosing to Pick an FTP Site shows you the folders and files that are part of the collection.

Once you find the book you are looking for, click its title to download it. In most cases, you can choose to download a file with either the TXT or ZIP extension. ZIP files are smaller but you have to unzip them before you can read their contents.

The Etext Archives

Another interesting site for free books is The Etext Archives at `http://www.etext.org`. This site offers documents in these categories: e-Zines (online magazines), politics, fiction, religion, and poetry. The collection isn't as large or varied as Project Gutenberg, but it contains some very interesting items.

You can also access the book collection formally held at `quartz.Rutgers.edu`.

There are plenty of other places on the Internet to get free material to read. Check out this one from Yahoo: `http://dir.yahoo.com/Arts/Humanities/Literature/Electronic_Literature/Collections`.

27 Solve Downloading Problems

Can't find that downloaded file? Get knocked offline before you're finished? Join the club! Downloading can be a rewarding experience, but it can also be frustrating. You'll find some answers here.

Downloading Problem Solving

Downloading can be like eating potato chips. Once you start, it is difficult to stop. If you're not careful, you can forget to note the location where downloaded files are being saved or their file name. Then, when you want to run the program, you don't know where to find it. That's bad. In this section, you'll learn how to use free programs to solve your downloading problems. That's good.

Here's What You Need

You need access to the Internet, and a program to help you download software. You'll either have to download one from the Internet, or use one of the two that are on the CD with this book: Download Assistant and GetRight.

Sites and Features

Within no time, you may find that you're downloading more and more programs. It is easy to get hooked on the convenience of getting software over the Internet, especially after you encounter the tremendous variety of material available. As a result, you may run into some problems. Downloading does have its downside, if you'll excuse the pun. Sometimes it gets difficult to find where you saved the downloaded program, and occasionally you'll get disconnected in the middle of downloading.

Even though the Save As box appears and asks for the name and the location of the downloaded file, it gets too easy to just click Save without making a note of the filename and location. I've done it, as have most folks in their downloading career. Once the file is in and you are offline, you realize you have no idea how to find it.

You can't search for the file using the Find feature because you don't know its file name. Sometimes, the name of the file has no apparent relationship to the name of the program. The alternatives are to start scanning all of your folders for something that looks right, or you could begin downloading the file all over again, and this time do it correctly.

The second big problem with downloading files, especially large ones, is the chance of getting disconnected in the middle of the download. There's something so frustrating about waiting for a 10-megabyte file to arrive, only to be disconnected.

No worries, you're in luck. There are scores of programs out there that can help. There are programs that help you organize your files for easy retrieval and automatically pick up where you left off if you were accidentally disconnected.

Some of the programs that you'll find include Download Wonder from `http://www.forty.com`; Download Butler from `http://www.lincolnbeach.com`; and Download Minder from `http://www.zedsoftware.com`.

If you do some searching in any software collection, you'll find dozens more.

Two helpful programs (Download Assistant and GetRight) are included on the CD with this book. Let's look at them a little more closely so you get the idea of how they can help. Both of these programs operate the same general way. They monitor your online activity and wait for a file to be downloaded. They then become active, substituting their own download features for those of your browser. If you have a virus protection program installed, both of these programs can use it to scan incoming files for virus.

Download Assistant

Download Assistant helps you keep track of your files by saving them in one of three groups of folders—Programs, Research, or Internet—all within the `C:\Program Files\Iolo` path. Each of these three folders is, in turn, divided into other folders. For example, the `C:\Program Files\IOLO\Programs` path contains folders named Productivity, Games, Utilities, and Applications. You'll find the program on the accompanying CD or you can down it from `http://www.iolo.com`.

After you install the Download Assistant, the Configuration Wizard begins. It scans your system for virus protection software and installed browsers. It asks you to choose which browser you want to use the program with and if you want to scan downloaded files with your virus protection software. You can also choose to have the program automatically open each file after it is downloaded.

To use the program, start it first and then open your browser. Whenever you start to download a file, the Download a File window appears, as shown in Figure 27.1. The information in the Download Description, File Source, and Specify a Filename for this Download text boxes appear automatically. You can use the other options in the dialog box to customize how you want the file downloaded.

FIGURE 27.1 Download a File window in Download Assistant

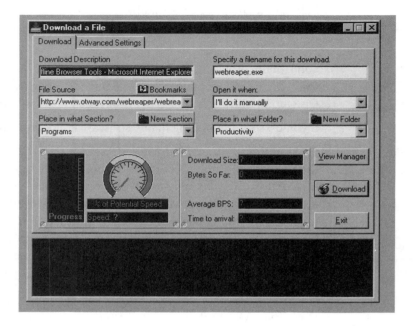

NOTE Each time you start the version of the program on the CD, you have to wait until the Continue Evaluation button is no longer dimmed before you can click it.

Advanced Settings tab Lets you choose to have Download Assistant automatically delete the file in 30 days, or ask if you want to delete the file if you have not opened, run, or installed the file in 10 days.

Place in what Section? Provides a selection of locations to which the file can be stored.

Place in what Folder? Provides a list of folders to which the file can be stored.

Open It When Either opens the program automatically after it is downloaded, or opens it only when you request it to be opened (choose between these two choices on the drop-down list).

Download button Begins the actual download. As the file comes over, you can watch its progress on the display to the left of the Download button. You'll see the total size of the file as well as the current number of downloaded bytes. This display also shows an approximate download speed and how much longer it will take. When the download is completed, a box appears reminding you of the section and folder.

View Manager button Takes you to the main screen of the Download Assistant (see Figure 27.2).

FIGURE 27.2 View Manager

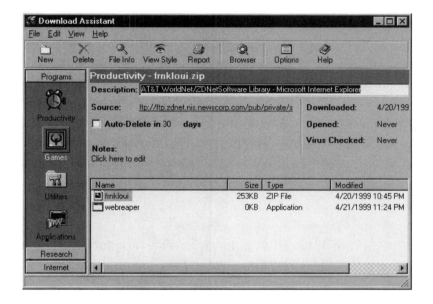

Along the left of the window are four groups. Click the group to display its folders, and then click a folder to list the files contained within it. In the main part of the window, you can select a file to see when it was downloaded, opened, and virus checked. You can also turn on the AutoDelete option. Use the menu bar to choose from these options:

New Creates a new section and folder.

Delete Deletes a section or folder.

File Info Displays the properties of the select file.

View Style Lets you change the way files are listed.

Report   Lets you print or save a report summarizing your downloaded programs.

Browser   Launches your Web browser.

Options   Opens a dialog box for customizing the way the program looks and operates.

In addition to the options listed above, consider the following actions.

◆ To run a program from the Download Assistant, just double-click it.

◆ To delete a file, right-click it, choose Delete from the shortcut menu, and then choose to either move the file to the Recycle Bin or permanently delete it.

You can also control Download Assistant by right-clicking the icon in the system tray to see these options:

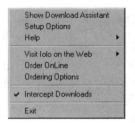

Turn off the Intercept Downloads option if you do not want the program to handle downloading chores.

GetRight

GetRight is a shareware program that can be downloaded from `http://www.getright.com`. In addition to its other functions, GetRight maintains a list of popular software collection sites. If there is a problem downloading the file, it can search for an alternate location from which to download the file.

You can also set GetRight to download files at a certain time (such as when you're sleeping), hang up, and turn off your computer when it is done (if your computer offers that feature).

When you first install the program, it takes you through a series of screens to configure it for your system. The installation program then places an icon in the system tray. Use the icon to control GetRight features or to open the GetRight Monitor dialog box on the desktop.

You can download a file by dragging the link to it onto the dialog box referred to as the GetRight monitor. Otherwise, when you start to download a file, the GetRight Save As box opens. In this box, you should check the name of the file, and choose a location. You can also use an FTP search to search for an alternate location. When you click Save, a progress window appears. This window shows the address of the program source and the location where the file is being stored. There is a running count of the number of bytes that have been downloaded, how much more time the download will take, and the speed at which it is downloading.

From the icon in the system tray, you can also open the Status box. This box shows the same basic information, but it shows it for all of files that have been downloaded. The buttons in the toolbar are shown here:

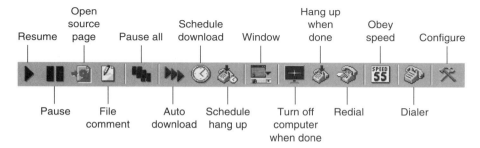

Use the toolbar and menu options to control and schedule downloads.

Finding the Endless Supply of Free Stuff

The Internet is just full of free offers. Some are totally free, others have quite a few strings attached to them. If you have the time to surf, read all of the offers, and respond to them, do so. You can save quite a lot of money on the Internet—enough to pay for your monthly ISP charge!

Get Discounts and Samples Galore!

Manufacturers are always trying to find a way to get you to buy their products. Some do it with a way in which most people are familiar—coupons and free offers. Clip a coupon out of the paper, hand it to the cashier at the store, and get some money off in return. With the Internet, you no longer have to cut coupons from the paper. You can just print or download coupons, and get free merchandise of all types.

Here's What You Need

All you need is access to the Internet!

Sites and Features

There are scores of sites offering coupons and free merchandise, but a few rise to the top. Supermarkets.com is a particularly good site.

Web Bucks

We all have to shop for food, paper goods, and other household items. Coupons help by giving us money off products that we purchase. Some stores even double the value of manufacturer's coupons, giving you 50 cents off for a 25-cent coupon. Whether or not you clip and use coupons, however, you can get money back from your shopping trip at many of the larger supermarket chains by printing a Value Page from http://www.supermarkets.com.

Here's how it works.

1. You print a page of money-back offers, called a Value Page, which includes a UPC code for each market.

2. When you go shopping, before starting to check out, have the cashier scan the UPC code into their system.

3. For each item on the Value Page that you purchase, you get a printed coupon called a Web Buck.

4. During your next shopping trip, you use the Web Buck coupons just like cash **on any product** you buy, whether or not that product is on the Value Page.

So let's say the Value Page has an offer for $1.00 if you purchase a specific brand of cereal. When you check out, you'll get a $1.00 coupon to use on anything on your next visit—it's just like cash.

If you have a manufacturer's coupon in addition to the Value Page offer, it's even better. While you cannot use two coupons for the same product, you can use a coupon when you purchase the cereal; you can still show the cashier the Value Page offer, and you will still be able to use the Web Buck you receive on your next visit. So, a 50-cent coupon and a $1.00 Web Buck actually gets you $1.50 off over two trips, or $2.00 off if your market doubles manufacturer's coupons.

Now, for the instructions to get your Value Page. Go to `http://www.supermarkets.com`. Enter your zip code and click the Submit Your Zip Code button to see a list of particpating supermarkets in your area.

Click the market that you use for shopping to see the total amount available in Web Bucks. You will also be able to customize your Value Page at this screen. For example, you can choose to eliminate baby and pet items, if you're not interested in these products. You can also enter your e-mail address, if you want to receive a weekly reminder to print out the Value Page.

When you click Get My Value Page, the page appears with the market's UPC code and a list of items that are currently on special. Print the Value Page, which is actually four or five pages long, and take it to the market on your next trip.

When you get your Web Bucks on that trip, store them in a safe location until you visit the supermarket again. You will then be able to use the Web Bucks like cash. You can also print out a new Value Page for that week to get additional Web Bucks for the items you buy.

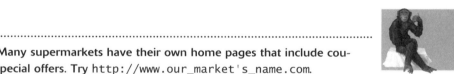

NOTE Many supermarkets have their own home pages that include coupons and special offers. Try `http://www.our_market's_name.com`.

The Mothers of All Free Sites

You can spend countless hours scouring the Web for free offers, or you can go to one of the sites that have a collection of free offers and links to even more free stuff. A few of the hottest freebie collections are listed here:

◆ `http://www.crecon.com/home/free5.html`
◆ `http://www.freestuffcentral.com`
◆ `http://www.4free.net`

Two collections that are outstanding are at `http://www.snap.com` (snap.com) and `http://www.gsmenter.com` (GSM Enterprises). At both of these sites, you can sign up for free samples of all kinds, and for special offers and promotions that don't require a single coupon. Just ask for the free stuff, sit back, and wait until it arrives at your mailbox.

Once you're at `http://www.snap.com`, click the *Free Stuff* link in the Online Shopping section. Once the new page appears, click the *Free Samples & Coupons* link to see a list of choices.

NOTE   You can go directly to the free stuff by pointing your browser at `http://www.snap.com/main/channel/item/0,4,-4553,00.html?st.sn .fdos.0.sh-fs`.

Each of the links on the Free Samples & Coupons page takes you to a free offer or list of offers that you can sign up to receive. The *Mousepads* link, for example, accesses a site that gives away mousepads with company logos or advertisements. Just click a link you're interested in, and follow the instructions that appear on-screen to get a free sample.

For even more free stuff, go to `http://www.gsmenter.com/dailyfreebie/ samples.htm`. Follow the link of your choice to sign up for free samples and other merchandise offers.

Enhancing the Internet Experience

The Internet is great, but it can always be better. In this part of the book, you'll learn how you can make the Internet faster, how to cut down on the advertisements, and how to share a single phone line and modem by networking your home.

29 Using Windows to Speed Browsing

No matter how fast your connection, sometimes it just takes time to download a Web site. Rather than waiting with nothing to do while a page comes in, wouldn't you rather read another Web page? This way, by the time you're done reading, the other site will be loaded and ready. You can even look at two or more sites at the same time!

Two Windows Are Better Than One!

If you are reading one site and you see a link you will want to go to, you can start downloading the linked page while you finish reading. This trick makes it so you have another browser window open. One window will download its page in the background while you are reading the other. This has the added advantage of letting you quickly return to the original page when you're done reading the second.

Here's What You Need

You won't need anything other than your trusty Web browser. For extra browsing features, however, consider using a program called FourTimes, which you'll find on the CD with this book.

Sites and Features

The capability to use multiple windows is already built into Windows and the Web browsers designed for it (Microsoft Internet Explorer and Netscape

Navigator). If you are using either of these browsers, here is how to view more than one site at a time.

◆ In Microsoft Internet Explorer, press Ctrl+N or select File ➤ New ➤ Window.

◆ In Netscape Navigator, select File ➤ New ➤Navigator Window.

This opens another window with the same Web site; in this new window, navigate to the other site you want to display. Each browser window will contain different sites now, and you'll now see two items for the browser in the Windows taskbar. As the new page is downloading, click the button for the original page on the Windows taskbar and continue reading. The site will continue to load even though its window is in the background.

As you can see, it is easy to switch back and forth between the two windows by clicking their button in the taskbar. You can also use standard Windows techniques to tile both windows so they are viewed at the same time, as shown in Figure 29.1.

FIGURE 29.1 **Displaying multiple browser windows**

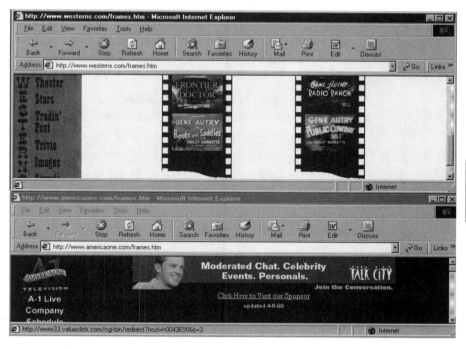

NOTE Though you can have more than two windows open, this is not advised because you'll start stretching the resources of your system.

If the browser windows are not already full screen, just drag each by a corner to the size you want it. You can place them top-and-bottom, as shown in Figure 29.1, or side-by-side. Side-by-side windows do not work as well because you'll have to scroll too much to read their contents.

If the windows are full screen, click the Restore button in the right side of the title bar in the foreground window. This makes it a smaller window so you can access its corners to drag. Then do the same for the remaining full-screen window.

Four Web Sites at One Time

If you are feeling the need to take this technique to an even higher level, run a wonderful little program called FourTimes. You'll find a copy of FourTimes on the CD with this book, or you can download it `http://members.tripod.com/~fourtimes`.

FourTimes lets anyone with Internet Explorer 4 and later (sorry, it doesn't work with other browsers) easily navigate through four pages at the same time (see Figure 29.2).

When you start FourTimes, you'll see four empty browser windows. Each window contains all the typical browser buttons. FourTimes may automatically connect to the Internet to download a default set of pages.

Just pick a window, enter the address of the site you want to display, and press Enter or click the Home button. Load a different Web site in each of the windows. You can even drag and drop links between panels. If you see a link you want to open, but you don't want it to replace the current page, just drag it to one of the other windows. FourTimes opens the linked page in that window.

In addition to the toolbar, FourTimes provides most of the common browser functions in its menu bar. You can use the View menu to access Internet Options and Preferences, the Tools menu to launch your e-mail and news programs, and the Favorites menu to add and organize bookmarks.

The Four menu is something you won't have seen before, and it is really interesting. If you have a combination of pages that you use periodically, you can use the Four menu to designate them as a group. You can then quickly access all four pages by just selecting the group name.

FIGURE 29.2   Reading four pages at once with FourTimes

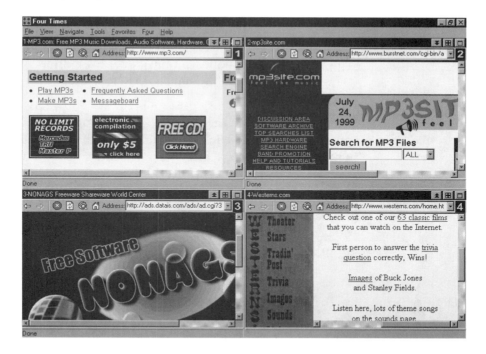

You can either create a group by entering the address of each site or by loading in each site's window ahead of time. For example, once you have one to four sites in the FourTimes windows, select Four ➢ Add to open this dialog box:

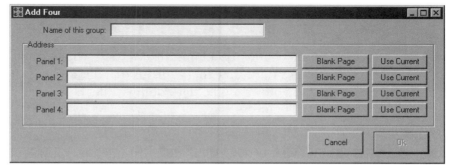

First, type a name for the group, and then follow these steps for each of the four windows:

1. Click Use Current to add the currently open site to the group.

2. Click Blank Page to make the window blank.

3. Type in the address of the site.

4. Finally, click OK.

Using the same technique, you can create any number of groups, each with its own name and combination of up to four sites.

If you later need to change the group, select Four ➤ Organize to see a list of your group names in the Organize Four dialog box. Click the group you want to change, and click Properties in the dialog box. Make any changes in the box that appears, and then click OK.

When you want to load the sites in a group, select Four ➤ Open. A bar appears down the left of the screen showing the group names. Just click the group you want to display. When you are finished with whatever changes you need to make, click the Back button on top of the bar to remove the group names from the screen.

30 Speed Up the Internet

Ever wonder what your computer is doing between the time you enter in a Web site name and the time page begins to appear on your screen? Get ready to find out!

Make Your Web Browsing Go Faster

When you enter the address of a Web site, you may notice a message in the browser's status line that explains that it is looking for the site. Knowing what the browser is actually doing while the message appears can help you speed up surfing.

Here's What You Need

In order to proceed, you will need your Web browser, an Internet connection, and FastNet99 or SpeedyNet, two handy programs.

Sites and Features

No matter how fast your modem, sometimes browsing the Web seems to take forever. If you already have the fastest modem available, and you don't want to go to the expense of a special phone line or cable modem, you can still speed up your connection.

All Web site names are identified by an Internet Protocol (IP) address. The name www.microsoft.com, for example, is located at the IP address 207.68.131.62. When you type a site name into your browser's location or address box, the browser has to first find the IP address before it can actually go to that site.

NOTE If you know the IP address of the site you want, enter it into the browser instead of the URL to speed things up.

Windows 98/NT maintains a file on your disk containing the IP addresses and names of sites that you visited on the Internet. The file is called Hosts (without any extension), and it is in the `C:\Windows` folder in Windows 98, and the `C:\WinNT\System32\Drivers\Etc\Hosts` folder in Windows NT. The Hosts file is a plan text file that you can open and look at with a word processing program.

If that file doesn't contain the IP address of a new Web site you are looking for, your browser checks a similar but much larger file at your ISP called a Domain Name Service (DNS) lookup. If the DNS file does not contain the IP address, one of several master DNS files maintained by organizations around the world is checked. Each of these steps takes some time.

To speed up the process of finding domain names, you can run one of several programs that let you manipulate the host list. Two such programs, FastNet99 and SpeedyNet, are on this book's CD.

FastNet99

FastNet99, which can also be downloaded at `http://members.xoom.com/gcriaco`, works in the background when your connection is idle. It looks up and verifies the IP address of sites in your Favorites or Bookmarks lists. You can also add IP addresses manually to FastNet99, if you know them, and otherwise manage the host file. This program also verifies each IP address to confirm that it is correct by going to the sites to make sure the address is still valid.

Starting FastNet99 opens the window shown in Figure 30.1. To look up an IP address from a domain name, follow these steps:

1. Click the Find IP option button.
2. Enter the Web site URL in the text box.
3. Click OK.

NOTE If you see three boxes in which to enter the server name, your copy of FastNet99 is set for three entry fields. You can change to a single box by clicking the Options tab and turning off the option labeled Data Entry with 3 Fields.

To locate a site name if you already have the IP address, follow these steps:

1. Click the Find URL option button.
2. Enter the IP address in the text box.
3. Click OK.

FIGURE 30.1 FastNet99

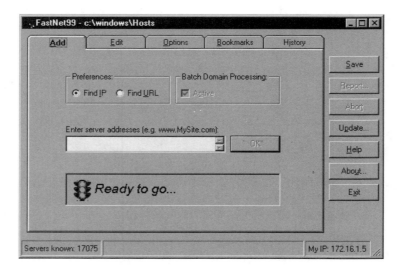

FastNet99 first checks the Hosts file (mentioned earlier) to see if the site is already listed. If it is, a message appears telling you so. Otherwise, FastNet99 connects to the Internet through your ISP and locates the information you are searching for. When the word Done appears in place of Ready to Go, click Save to add the information to the Hosts file.

The Edit tab in the FastNet99 window lets you view the entries in the Hosts file, verify that they are accurate, and remove duplicates.

Use the Options tab to fine tune how FastNet99 works. For example, enable the Data Entry with 3 Fields option to change the text box on the Add tab to this:

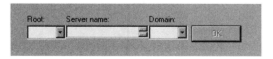

You can then enter the site name in three segments, and you will be able to maintain a list of up to ten entries for each. Here are the three segments:

Root   Is the prefix, such as www or ftp.

Server name   Is the company name, as in Microsoft, Netscape, or Lycos.

Domain   Identifies the type of the site, as in com, org, or edu.

With this option active, you can also select or deselect the Batch Domain Processing check box on the Add tab. Batch processing will search for all variations of the domain, and any combination of the root, server name, and domains.

The Monthly Batch Function choices on the Options tab let you have FastNet99 form any of these four tasks at the start of each month:

Verify All   Checks to make sure that all IP addresses are still correct for the domain names.

Scan Bookmarks   Ensures that each entry in the Bookmark list has a valid IP address.

Scan History   Ensures that each entry in the History list has a valid IP address.

Update   Checks for a FastNet99 update.

SpeedyNet

SpeedyNet also lets you manage the Hosts list using the interface shown in Figure 30.2. You will also find this program on the CD, or you can download it from http://www.comcen.com.au/~netwiz/software/snet4.

FIGURE 30.2 SpeedyNet

To add an IP address, follow these steps:

1. Click the Add/Modify Server option button.

2. Enter the URL of the site.

3. Click Go.

Use the Import button in the SpeedyNet window to add the sites from your Internet Explorer favorites and Netscape Navigator bookmarks. The View Site options displays the contents of the Hosts file so you can delete or verify specific entries. Use the Verify All button to verify the entire Hosts file.

31 More Ways to Speed Up the Internet

In addition to DNS lookups that you learned about in the last section, there are all sorts of way to speed up your Internet experience.

Make Your Web Browsing Go Even Faster

Wherever you have creative minds, you'll find people trying to do things better and faster. There is no shortage of creativity on the Internet, so you shouldn't be surprised that there are plenty of ways to surf the Internet more quickly.

Here's What You Need

You will need your Web browser, an Internet connection, and LinkFox and BoostWEB, handy programs you'll find on the CD of this book.

Sites and Features

In this section, we'll look at two different approaches:

◆ Preloading pages onto your computer's hard disk

◆ Compressing information though a proxy server

Programs to help you get started experimenting with each of these techniques are on the accompanying CD.

Preloading Web Sites Using LinkFox

The longest delays in browsing occur when you're waiting for a Web page to download to your computer. Rather than using multiple windows, which take up a lot of your computer's resources, you can preload a page into your computer's hard disk. This process is called *caching*. It is much faster to load a page into the cache file than into a hidden browser window. After preloading a site, the process of downloading will take almost no time at all. The information will just be loaded from the cache into the window later on.

LinkFox is a program that lets you select pages to preload into the cache. You'll find LinkFox on the CD or you can download it from `http://www` `.hageltech.com`.

After LinkFox is installed, you can start the program from the icon it places in your system tray, but it will start automatically when your browser connects to the Internet.

LinkFox can take three forms—a full window, a small window, and an icon on the desktop called a drop box.

To select a view, right-click the icon in the system tray and choose the view from the menu that appears. Right-click the LinkFox icon in the system tray and choose Options to select a default view.

Before reading a Web page in detail, scan the page and look for links that you will be interested in seeing. Drag the links from the Web page to the LinkFox window or Drop Basket. Now, as you are reading the page, LinkFox downloads the linked pages to the computer's cache.

If you drag the link to the window, you'll see a small disk icon in the LinkFox window as the file is being downloaded and saved. A checkmark will then appear to indicate each page that has been successfully completed. If the site cannot be loaded, a red X appears next to its name.

When you're ready to read one of the pages, double-click it or select it and press Enter. You can also right-click it and choose Open in New Window from the shortcut menu.

If you drag the link to the Drop Basket, the chain image will turn yellow as the link is downloading. It will then turn green when it is finished. If the site cannot be loaded, the chain turns red. To open a site, right-click the Drop Basket and choose either Show Full Window or Show Link List Only from the shortcut menu.

By default, the links are deleted from LinkFox when you exit the program. To retain a link so you can open the page at a later time, right-click it and choose Persistent Link from the shortcut menu.

Cutting Download Time with BoostWEB

A different approach to speeding up the Web can be found using BoostWEB. You'll find a copy of this program on the CD, or you can download it from `http://www.boostweb.net`. (Note that the evaluation version of BoostWEB provides 14 days of free service. An annual subscription is required to continue the service.) BoostWEB actually inserts itself between your computer and the Web sites that you want to download.

Installing the program places a virtual BoostWEB client on your computer. When you connect to the Web, information downloaded to your computer is channeled through the BoostWEB server computer. Before the server sends the page to your computer, it compresses the information for faster transmission.

As you browse, you'll see a window like the one shown in Figure 31.1. The percentages in the window show you the average compression rate (on the top) and the maximum rate. The higher the number, the more efficient the compression, and the more time is being saved. In Figure 31.1, for example, the average rate is 76%, roughly meaning that you're getting the page in only 24% of the time it would take if you were not using the program.

The other graphs on the page show how various types of elements are being compressed, and the compression as data flows, read from left to right.

FIGURE 31.1   **BoostWEB**

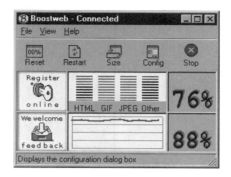

In order to use BoostWEB, your browser must be set up to use a *proxy server*. A proxy server is an intermediary through which information flows. Here are the steps for setting up the proxy server in Microsoft Internet Explorer.

1. Right-click the Internet Explorer icon on the desktop and choose Properties, or go to the Windows Control Panel and open Internet Options.

2. Click the Connections tab.

3. Click your dial-up connection and then click Settings.

4. Enable the Use a Proxy Server check box.

5. Click Advanced.

6. In the http section, under Proxy Address to Use, enter **Localhost**.

7. Enter **6724** under Port.

8. Make sure the other options are cleared.

9. Make sure to clear the check box labeled Use the Same Proxy Server for All Protocols.

10. Click OK until you return to the desktop or to the Control Panel.

If you are using Netscape Navigator 4, use these steps to set the proxy server.

1. Start Netscape Navigator.

2. Choose Edit ➤ Preferences. In some earlier versions of Netscape, you have to choose Options ➤ Network ➤ Proxies.

3. Click Advanced and then click Proxies.

4. Select the Manual Proxy Configuration option button and then click View.

5. In the http section, under Address of Proxy Server to Use, enter **Localhost**.

6. Enter **6724** under Port.

7. Click OK.

32 Monitor Your Connection

Keep an eye on your network connections to find the best time to get files and surf the Web. In order to do so, read the following information.

Keep Track of Your Actual Connection Speed

Even though your modem is advertised as 56K, it doesn't mean you're actually downloading and uploading that fast. By monitoring the actual connection speeds, you can determine the best time to connect and download files.

Here's What You Need

In order to do this, you will need your Web connection and Windows Dial-Up Networking or a program on the CD with this book.

Sites and Features

You can connect to the Internet using Windows Dial-Up Networking and still monitor your connection speeds.

One of the easiest ways is to run a program designed to display a small window that reports connection speed as you work. DU Meter, on the CD with this book or downloaded from http://www.hageltech.com, can perform this function. Running the program displays an icon in the system tray and a small box, as shown here:

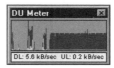

The box stays in the foreground as you surf the Internet showing the actual download time (for information coming to your computer) and upload time (information from your computer to the Internet).

Hide or redisplay the box by right-clicking the system tray icon. Right-click the icon and choose Manual Hide from the shortcut menu to remove the DU Meter box from the screen. Click the tray icon again to restore the box.

Choose Options from the shortcut to customize DU Meter. Use the Window Properties tab of the Options dialog box to adjust how the meter appears, how times are reported, and the color of lines on the graph. The Network Interface tab lets you choose what connections to monitor. By default, DU Meter keeps track of your modem and LAN connections. You can use the tab to specify one connection to watch and ignore the other.

The Graph Scale tab of the dialog box lets you set the upper limit of the scale—the maximum value of the y-axis. The options on the Graph Scale tab are

Automatic Scale Update   Adjusts the scale to accommodate the highest transfer rates.

Pre-defined Values   Sets the upper limit of the scale to the speed of your modem.

Manual Setup   Lets you specify the upper range.

Use the Notifications tab to have DU Meter warn you, or disconnect you, when the connection reaches a minimum value. The Ticker feature plays a sound when a set number of bytes are downloaded, giving you an audible representation of the transfer speed.

The Totals option on the DU Meter shortcut menu opens a box reporting the total number of bytes uploaded and downloaded. You can choose to reset the number to start counting from zero.

The StopWatch option lets you track the transfer rate over a specific period. Right-click the system tray icon and choose StopWatch. Click Start when you want to begin monitoring the transfer rate. Click Stop—which replaces the Start button—to stop the counter.

33 Get Help Connecting

The Dial-Up Networking feature of Windows is easy to use, but it has no frills. It dials your ISP, but that's all. You can get your dial-up connection to do a lot more with a little help from our online friends.

Make Connecting Easier

In *It's About Time* earlier in this book, you learned how to keep track of your online time by using programs that you can download from the Internet. These programs acted as an intermediary between you and Windows Dial-Up Networking. There are all sorts of other programs that expand on Windows Dial-Up Networking.

Here's What You Need

You'll need your browser, ISP, and some free or inexpensive software. Some of this software can be found on the CD that comes with this book, other products will need to be downloaded from the Internet.

Sites and Features

Programs abound that let you control your online sessions and help you connect more easily. In fact, you set up these programs so you can connect through them rather than through Windows Dial-Up Networking. Instead of opening your browser, start one of these programs and connect through it to access its features.

Most of these programs offer a variety of functions that can be found separately in other software (such as Whois, Ping, and Trace Route). Like software that we have already discussed, these programs keep track of online time and cost, and keep your connection alive. By using one of these programs, however, you get all of these features and more in one place.

Some of the more popular programs in this category are

PROGRAM	DOWNLOAD LOCATION
Dunce	`http://www.vecdev.com`
CyberKit	`http://www.ping.be/cyberkit`
InterNet Anywhere Toolkit	`http://www.tnsoft.com`
Net Toolbox	`http://www.nettoolbox.com`
NetScan Tools	`http://www.nwpsw.com`
Network Toolbox	`http://www.jriver.com/products/network-toolbox.html`
Sam Spade	`http://www.blighty.com/products/spade`

We'll take a closer look at two such programs here—ConnectPal and Rascal.

Your Pal, ConnectPal

ConnectPal is a full-featured shareware program found on the accompanying CD, or downloadable from `http://www.connect-pal.com`. Use it to work between you and the Windows Dial-Up Networking feature. For example, you can set ConnectPal to automatically start other programs when you go online. You can launch an e-mail program, a downloading helper such as GetRight, another timer or cost-tracking program, an FTP application, or a program such as Microsoft Word.

When you first start the program you'll be asked to configure it using the dialog box shown in Figure 33.1.

Use the tabs of the dialog box to explore these functions.

Connection Sets up user profiles with name and passwords.

Cost Keeps track of free time and online charges.

Warnings Sets warnings to occur at cost and online time levels.

Options Customizes your online environment.

Mail Watch Sets the program to automatically look for new mail and news messages.

Statistics Shows records of online time, costs, and other calculations.

FIGURE 33.1 Configuring ConnectPal

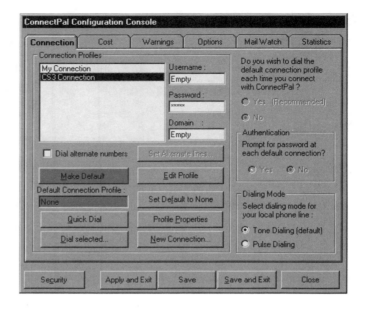

You first task is to set up a profile.

1. In the Connection profiles list, click the dial-up networking connection you want to use. If you need to create a new one, click New Connection to launch the Windows program that lets you create one.

2. Click the Edit Profile button to display this dialog box:

3. Enter your username and password. You must enter these in ConnectPal even though you may have already saved them when using Windows Dial-Up Networking. ConnectPal uses the phone number information from the Windows Dial-Up Networking profile but sends its own username and password when logging in.

4. Click the Modify button—the center button below the Domain text box.

5. If you have to change any of the settings in the dial-up networking connection, click profile Properties.

6. Click the dial-up connection you want to use and then click the Make Default button.

7. Use the Options tab to customize other aspects of the connection. For example, you can choose to:

◆ Dial your ISP as soon as you start ConnectPal.

◆ Start up to five other programs when you connect.

◆ Display online time information when connected.

◆ Keep your connection alive using up to three different methods— simulating e-mail (Post Office Protocol—POP main), requesting a Web site (Ping), or downloading software (FTP).

◆ Redial if disconnected.

8. Click Save and then Close.

Once you configure ConnectPal for the first time, you'll see the main program window, shown in Figure 33.2. To later change the configuration, click the C.C.C. button.

FIGURE 33.2 **ConnectPal window**

Use the Connect button to dial into the connection you established in the configuration as the default profile. Once you make the connection, you can start your Web browser, e-mail program, or any other application for which you want to use your Internet connection. The Speed button makes the connection without prompting for your username or password. The Launch button lets you select up to 10 programs to launch manually.

If you make your Internet connection before starting ConnectPal, click the Scan button. ConnectPal will detect the connection, start timing it, and apply your selected options, such as launching additional programs.

The Net Tools button accesses four common Internet features.

- ◆ **Whois**   Lets you look up the registered owner of a Web site.

- ◆ **Finger**   Lets you check to see if a friend is online, if their ISP supports this feature.

- ◆ **Time**   Lets you access Greenwich Meridian Time.

- ◆ **Get Host**   Lets you get the domain name of an IP address, and vice versa.

When you disconnect with ConnectPal, you'll be asked to confirm the action in this message:

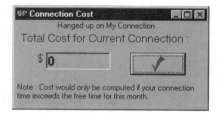

You Rascal, You

Another popular connection management program is Rascal, which you can download from `http://www.basta.com`. Rascal also acts as your dial-up connection and includes automatic reconnection and keep-alive functions. The Rascal window is shown in Figure 33.3.

Rascal uses the default dial-up networking connection, but before dialing, you have to click the Session tab and enter your username and password.

At the bottom left of the Sessions tab is the Dial button. Click this button when you want to connect to your ISP. After making the connection, you can start your Web browser or e-mail program.

FIGURE 33.3   Rascal window

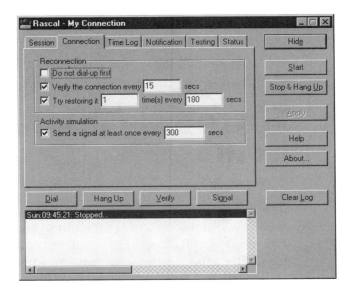

Use the Reconnect options on the Connection tab to determine how Rascal monitors and reacts to your connection status:

Do Not Dial Up First   If you are disconnected, Rascal will not reconnect, but it will wait until you connect with some other programs before monitoring the connection.

Verify the Connection   This specifies what intervals Rascal checks to see if you are connected or offline. This option must be turned on in order to use the Activity Simulation feature to keep your connection active.

Try Restoring It   This specifies how often Rascal will attempt to reconnect, and the interval between attempts.

Use the Activity simulation setting to keep your signal alive by pinging the ISP at regular intervals. Enable the check box and then enter the number of seconds between pings in the text box.

N O T E   To manually send a ping to the ISP, click the Signal button. Click Verify to check your connection status.

Use the other tabs of the Rascal window to time your sessions and keep track of online costs, to play sounds when you connect and disconnect, to test Rascal by simulation connections and disconnections, and to display connection status information such as your ISP's address and name.

34 There's No Place Like Home

Most ISPs give you a home page—a starting location that your browser first opens when you connect to the Internet. You shouldn't feel locked into their home page if it doesn't give you everything you want. Some other ISP might offer more features—you can take advantage of them even if you are not a member.

Changing Your Home Page

ISPs try to offer a wide range of features in their home page. Some of the items are for members only, such as links to support help. However, most of the links in a home page can be used by anyone, whether they are members or not, so keep your eyes open for another ISP home page that is better for you. There are even home pages that aren't provided by ISPs.

Here's What You Need

You won't need anything special, except access to the Internet and the knowledge to set your home page, which is provided here. You set the home page within your browser. That's how it knows the page to open when first launched and where to go when you click the Home button on the browser's toolbar.

NOTE Some of the sites mentioned here have a link that will make it your home page automatically, but it is best to set the home page yourself to make sure it gets done right.

With Microsoft Internet Explorer, follow these steps when you want to change your home page:

1. Right-click the Internet Explorer icon on the desktop and choose properties. If you don't have an icon, try Start ➤ Settings ➤ Control Panel and open Internet Options. If the browser is already running, select Tools ➤ Internet Options.

2. In the General tab of the Internet Properties dialog box, shown in Figure 34.1, enter the address of the home page in the Address box.

3. Click OK.

FIGURE 34.1 **Changing the home page in Internet Explorer**

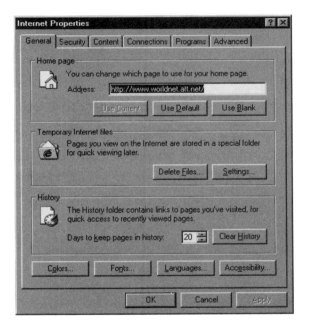

With Netscape Navigator, follow these steps to change the home page:

1. Launch Netscape.

2. Select Edit ➤ Preferences to open the Preferences dialog box.

3. Click the Navigator category if it is not already selected.

4. Enter the address of the home page in the Location text box.

5. Make sure the Navigator Starts With option is set to Home Page.

6. Click OK.

Sites and Features

In your search for the perfect home page, start by taking a look at the home pages for some of the nationwide ISPs, such as `http://www.aol.com`, `http://www.worldnet.att.net`, and `http://www.compuserve.com`.

The AOL home page offers links to categories it calls Web Centers. Click the link for the category that interests you and then continue browsing. The AOL home page also has lists of links classified as Shortcuts, Shopping, and Community, as well as a search engine using AOL NetFind. Just click the link you're interested in following.

The CompuServe home page offers the same Web Centers (which shouldn't be surprising since it is owned by AOL) as well as links to top news stories, stock prices, weather, and sport scores.

NOTE Click Main Menu under the Member Benefits section to get to a special area for CompuServe members only. You'll have to enter your CompuServe user number and password.

You should also consider `http://www.netscape.com`. The site is not just about Netscape the company—it offers a series of links by category as well as the top stories on `http://abcnews.go.com`, stock quotes from Citibank, and computing information.

Next, look at the home pages of these popular search engines:

◆ `http://www.lycos.com`
◆ `http://www.yahoo.com`
◆ `http://www.snap.com`

All of these sites provide a great starting point for browsing because they offer a variety of links to popular topics and services. In fact, their categories are almost identical, and much like the ones shown for Netscape. There are still enough differences between them that you should take your time to explore each one. You never know what special feature you'll find.

Why do these sites offer so many features? As I am sure you have heard before, advertising. The more hits the site gets, the more advertising revenue it can generate—sort of like free television. So it pays for a site to offer as many freebies and other enticements as possible.

There's so much possible revenue involved that there are sites that exist just to be homepages, such as `http://www.homepageware.com`.

When you log onto this site, you get a menu of current news links, as well as free and not-so-free offers, as shown in Figure 34.2. While most of the "free" offers are just that, you can't take all of the "free" offers too literally. Several links lead to sites and offers where some money is involved. The offers change periodically, so it pays to check back with homepageware .com regularly.

FIGURE 34.2 Homepageware's home page

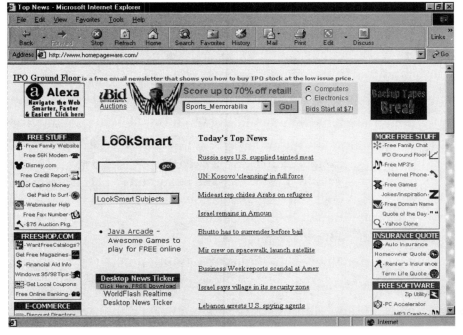

Creating a Custom Home Page on Excite

A number of the home page sites let you customize the page for your interests and tastes. They do so by letting you select options to display or by indicating your local area or other personal information. They then store the information as a cookie on your computer, and access the cookie when you log on to the site.

An example of this is `http://www.excite.com`. Excite is one of the most popular search engines, and its home page offers a wide variety of links and services. Most of the areas are labeled My, such as My Weather, My Sports, My Services, My Horoscope.

With My Horoscope, for example, you are prompted to enter your birthday, and then click Get My Horoscope. Excite adds the birth date to your cookie, so each time you log on, you get your personal horoscope.

For My Weather, you enter your zip code to get local weather conditions. For My Sports and My Services, along with free e-mail and other features, you have to sign up with Excite, but membership is FREE.

Click the link Personalize Your Page at the top of their home page, and then follow the on-screen instructions. You'll be asked to choose a user name and password, and enter your e-mail address, birth date, and zip code. Once you do, you'll be welcomed personally when you log on, you'll get local weather and your horoscope each time you connect to the site, and you will be able to change My Sports and My Services.

At the top of the My Sports section, for example, click the link Change to select which scores and games you are interested in, as well as the specific teams.

When you click Change under My Services, you select which links you want to appear there from a list of options the site provides.

Excite isn't the only service that offers a personal home page. AT&T WorldNet, Netscape, and many others let you create custom home pages once you sign on or become members.

Surfing the EZ Way

As another alternative to a home page, you can run the EZSurfer99 Portal that you'll find on the CD with this book. The program makes its site your home page.

The program actually installs most of the graphic elements of the home page on your hard disk. When you launch your browser, Windows connects to your ISP, quickly loads most of the home page from your disk, and then downloads any new EZSurfer features from its Web site, `http://www.ezsurfer.net`.

Just click any of the topics shown in the EZSurfer screen to get information or navigate to other locations.

....

NOTE If you delete EZSurfer from your computer, it still sets `http://www.ezsurfer.net` as your browser's home page.

35 Browsing Offline

After you wait for a site to come on your screen, it is really a shame to keep your phone tied up while you read it. The solution is to read the Web page after you've hung up the phone; this is called offline browsing.

Freeing Up Your Phone Line

One way to read a Web page offline is to print a copy of it and then read it after you've disconnected. The only problem is you can waste a lot of paper and time printing. That's when you download the site. You can then read the Web site even after you've disconnected from the Internet.

Here's What You Need

You'll need a free or inexpensive program you can download from the Internet or find on the CD with this book.

Sites and Features

Downloading the site lets you view it in your browser when you are offline exactly how it appears when you are online. You can also use programs that let you download more than one *level* of information. Each level represents the pages that the links on the original page would display. When you disconnect, you can then browse though the site offline.

Before we look at the programs that can perform this magic, let's look at how you use your Web browser offline.

The quickest way to read a Web page offline is to display it when you are online and select File ➤ Save As. In the dialog box that appears, set the location where you want the file stored on your disk—the desktop is the easiest place to access it—and click OK.

When you are ready to read the page offline, just find the Web page file using Windows Explorer, or use the My Computer icon on the desktop. Double-click the page to open it in the browser, which will remain offline.

You can also start your browser but cancel the connection so it does not dial in. The last downloaded copy of your home page might appear, or some message will appear saying that the site cannot be displayed. Next, choose Open from the File menu. In the box that appears, click Browse and locate the Web page you want to open. Double-click it to open it in the browser window.

NOTE Using the Save As command only gets the information that you see on the screen. There are often files associated with the Web site that you'd need on your disk to view the site offline exactly how it appears online.

The Programs

There are hundreds of programs that can download Web sites for offline browsing. We were fortunate enough to get two for inclusion on the CD. We'll look at both of these programs and then two other popular alternatives that you can download. For other programs, go to any of the software collections and search for the word "download."

Zip Up The Web   This handy program doesn't let you download levels of a site, but it is easy to use and very kind to your disk space. Zip Up The Web, which you'll find on the CD or you can download from `http://www.zipuptheweb.com`, saves a copy of the selected site as a compressed, self-executing program on your disk.

When you start Zip Up The Web, it dials your ISP and launches your Web browser. (The first time you start the program you have to go through the free registration process.) You'll then see the dialog box shown in Figure 35.1.

Then follow these steps:

1. Enter the address of the site you want to download in the first text box.

2. Enter the location and name of the resulting files on the second text box.

3. Click View URL in Browser if you need to confirm the site.

4. Click Click Here to ZIP.

FIGURE 35.1   Zip Up The Web

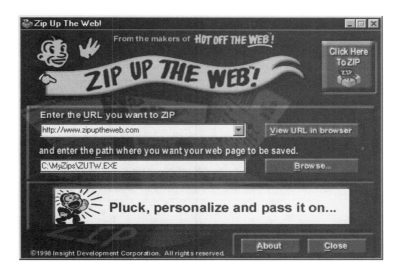

Zip Up The Web accesses the site and creates a program file in the My Zips folder, which will appear like this in Windows Explorer:

The file contains all of the text and graphics of the Web site, but it is compressed to take up as little disk space as possible. Because the file is actually an executable program, just double-click the file to display it in your Web browser.

Net Vampire   As another approach to downloading a Web site, try using Net Vampire, which is on the CD and can be downloaded from `http://www.netvampire.com`.

NOTE   If you like the version of NetVampire supplied on the CD, you can download the most recent version of the program from its Web site.

When you start Net Vampire it may dial into your ISP, so start it when you're ready to browse. The Net Vampire window is shown in Figure 35.2. You'll also see the Drop Basket, a small icon in the desktop that you can drag links to in order to download.

FIGURE 35.2   **Net Vampire window**

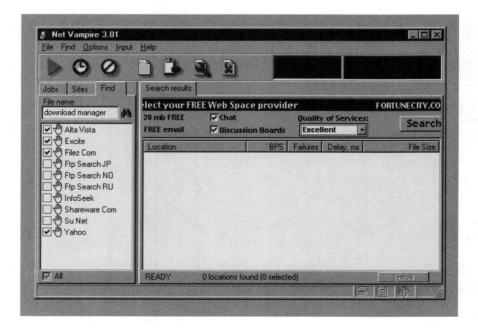

NOTE To make sure Net Vampire intercepts downloads, pull down its Input menu and enable the Monitor Browser Clicks option.

Start your browser. When you get to a site you want to save for offline viewing, follow these steps:

1. Select and copy its URL from the address box.

2. Switch to Net Vampire by clicking its icon in the Windows taskbar.

3. Click the Paste URLs from Clipboard button to open the dialog box shown in Figure 35.3. The address of the site appears in the Locations box.

FIGURE 35.3 Setting the location to download

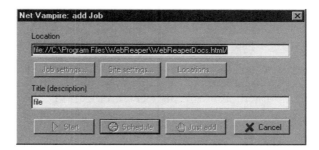

4. Click Start to download the site. You can also click Schedule if you want to download the site at a later time.

When you disconnect from the Internet, you'll find the Web site in the Program Files/Net Vampire folder. Open the file in your browser to view it offline.

You can also download a site without even displaying it when online. If you see that the link that appears looks interesting, hold down the ALT key and click the link, or drag the link to the Net Vampire Drop Basket. Net Vampire opens the Add Job dialog box with the URL in the Locations text box. Click Start to download the page. If you add the URL of a file from an FTP site, Net Vampire downloads the file, and can even resume where it left off if you get disconnected.

36 Staying Alive and Online

Most ISPs won't let you keep the line tied up for extended periods when you're not doing anything online. After some set number of minutes of inactivity—no browsing on your part—your ISP may disconnect you, or flash an on-screen message letting you know that you'll be disconnected in so many seconds.

Don't Let Your ISP Cut You Off

You may be called away from your computer while online, or just get pre-occupied doing something else. If you have to stay online during periods of inactivity, then here are some solutions.

Here's What You Need

You'll need your Web browser and Connection Keeper, which you can download from the CD with this book.

Sites and Features

While some users may consider this an annoyance, it is actually a very considerate policy to other users who are trying to get online. With unlimited service, it would be tempting for a user to stay online all day so they wouldn't have to encounter a busy signal. This practice just causes busy signals for others.

NOTE While programs that keep your connection alive are handy, be considerate of other users and disconnect if you'll be idle for any length of time.

With that said, if you have to go away from your computer and you need to remain online, there are plenty of programs to help you. These programs work by either pinging your ISP at regular intervals, or by sending requests for nonexistent or random Web sites. Your ISP thinks you're online and doesn't start the disconnect clock.

Connection Keeper

 You'll find one such program, Connection Keeper, on the CD with this book. Connection Keeper, which you can also download from `http://www.gammadyne.com`, is shown in Figure 36.1.

FIGURE 36.1   **Staying alive online with Connection Keeper**

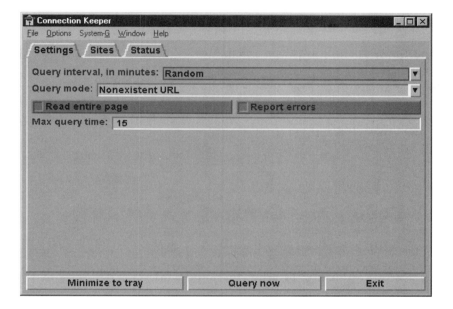

 Before you walk away from your computer, or fall asleep online, just start the program. It works in the background, sending queries for Web sites at either random or regular intervals that you control from the Query Interval list.

You can choose to have it ask for a nonexistent site or random sites from a built-in list. Use the Sites tab to review the list or to add others. If you choose random sites, you can also select from these options:

Read Entire Page   Downloads the entire page from the random Web site. With this option turned off, the site is just opened and closed but not actually downloaded.

Report Errors   Displays an on-screen message if an error occurs when a random site is being called.

Max Query Time   Is the time the program waits for a query to be completed.

If your ISP still disconnects you with Connection Keeper running, reduce the Query interval time, or click the Status tab and turn on the Auto-Reconnect option. With this option on, Connection Keeper will redial your ISP when you are disconnected.

Some other programs that will keep your connection alive are Stay Alive from `http://www.tfi-technology.com` and Auto-IP Publisher from `http://www.lakefield.net/~smiller/autoip`.

37 Trace Your Steps

Where does your computer go to get to that Web site? Your signals bounce around from computer to computer to bring it to you. Find out where your computer has gone!

Follow the Computer's Route

When you travel from your house to Grandma's, or to any other place for that matter, you make a lot of stops and turns along the way. So does your computer when you send it off to fetch a Web site. The Internet is really a whole bunch of computers linked together, so you can track down the route your computer took to get from one point to another.

Here's What You Need

All you will need is your Web browser and free programs that come with Windows. For even more features, use TJPing or Ping Plotter, both of which are included on the CD with this book. You may also download other shareware programs.

You'll also need to know a little about the way information is transported around the Internet.

Information is transmitted through the Internet in packets of data. The packets travel through a series of computers called Internet Protocol (IP) routers until they get to their destination. Every computer is connected to the Internet, and so every Web site has an IP address. The address is a series of numbers, something like 135.145.64.39, that uniquely identifies it. Your own computer will have an IP address as well.

Tracing programs work by sending several small packets of information called echo records, or pings, through the Internet. The ping includes a Time To Live (TTL) number. Each site that handles the message is supposed to decrease the TTL number by 1 before sending it on to the next site. When the TTL gets to 0, the site sends back a signal to the source that includes its IP address, and the time the round trip took as measured and displayed in milliseconds (1/1000 of a second). The lower the time, the better your connection.

The first ping the trace program sends includes a TTL number of 1. When the message gets to the first router, it subtracts 1 from it, sees that the number is now 0, and sends back a response. Your computer then sends another packet with a TTL of 2. This packet gets as far as the second router, which sends back a response with its IP address and time.

The pings continue until they are received and returned by the destination you specified. The TTL used to reach that site represents the number of "hops" the route takes. The round trip time (RTT) to this site is the actual time to the Web site.

By reporting each of the IP addresses that receive the pings, you get a complete picture of the route taken through the Internet.

Programs that send pings through the Internet will not wait forever for a response, so they have a time-out time. A time out means that after so many seconds the program gives up and stops.

Sites and Features

To get to a Web site, your browser has to hop from computer to computer until it reaches its destination so it can display it on your screen.

It's interesting to see the route your computer takes to get to a Web site. The number of stops it makes along the way and the places it goes might amaze you. But more than that, tracing the route can show you where some bottlenecks occur.

Ping and Tracert—Free with Windows

Windows comes with two free programs for tracking the route to any Web site: Ping and Tracert. You run these programs from the DOS command line rather than from a window, but they are easy to use.

The Ping program sends four pings to the Web site you specify so you can compare the response time for each. To use Ping, follow these steps.

1. Select Start ➢ Programs ➢ MS-DOS Prompt to open a DOS window.

2. Type **ping**, then a space, and enter the name of the Web site you want to go to. The command would appear like this: `ping www.worldnet .att.net`.

3. Press Enter.

The program will dial into your ISP, if you are not already connected, send pings to the site specified, and display the results. (See Figure 37.1, from my computer to `http://www.worldnet.att.net`, my ISP.)

FIGURE 37.1 Pinging a Web site

The Tracert command sends outs three packets and measures the time it takes to get to each IP address along the way. To use Tracert follow these steps.

1. Select Start ➢ Programs ➢ MS-DOS Prompt to open a DOS window.

2. Type **tracert**, then a space, and enter the name of the Web site you want to go to. The command would appear like this: `tracert www .sybex.com`

3. Press Enter.

The program will dial into your ISP, if you are not already connected, and send pings to trace the route. Figure 37.2 shows the trace from my computer to http://www.sybex.com. It shows the time it takes for each of the three packets, and the name and IP address of each stop.

FIGURE 37.2   Tracing the route to Sybex

```
MS-DOS Prompt                                            _ □ X

Auto    ▾    ☐ ▤ ▨ ▣ ▤ ▤ A

C:\WINDOWS>tracert www.sybex.com

Tracing route to www.sybex.com [206.100.29.83]
over a maximum of 30 hops:

  1    152 ms    142 ms    177 ms   199.70.67.39
  2    168 ms    155 ms    160 ms   1.philadelphia-06-07rs.pa.dial-access.att.net [1
2.78.210.1]
  3    261 ms    193 ms    169 ms   199.70.127.21
  4    195 ms    163 ms    200 ms   br2-a350s6.n54ny.ip.att.net [12.127.11.101]
  5    149 ms    193 ms    185 ms   gr1-a3100s1.n54ny.ip.att.net [192.205.31.245]
  6    148 ms    180 ms    152 ms   204.70.10.146
  7    271 ms    235 ms    268 ms   corerouter1.SanFrancisco.cw.net [204.70.9.131]
  8    226 ms    238 ms    301 ms   core2.SanFrancisco.cw.net [204.70.4.201]
  9    252 ms    243 ms    262 ms   border7-fddi-0.SanFrancisco.cw.net [204.70.158.5
1]
 10    298 ms    269 ms    358 ms   wlinet-sf.SanFrancisco.cw.net [204.70.161.70]
 11   wlinet-sf.SanFrancisco.cw.net [204.70.161.70]  reports: Destination net unr
eachable.

Trace complete.

C:\WINDOWS>
```

NOTE   To make Tracert go faster, add –d after the command so the name of each site is not reported, just the IP address.

Running TJPing

Rather than work with the DOS command prompt, you can use the freeware program TJPing to trace a route and more. You'll find the program on the CD with this book, and you can download it from http://www.topjimmy.net/tjs.

TJPing provides several useful functions:

PING   Sends a signal to let you know if the site is valid and can be reached. It also tells you the RTT and the TTL—the time of the round trip and the number of hops.

TRACE   Traces the route the IP packets take to get to the site.

LOOKUP   Finds the site's name if you enter its IP address, and vice versa.

Start the program to see the window in Figure 37.3. Type the name of the site or its IP address, and click the function you want to perform.

FIGURE 37.3   TJPing

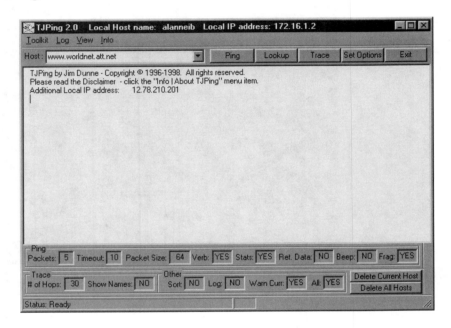

By default, the trace option shows the IP address and round trip time, but not the name of each router.

To display the names, and set other options, click the Set Options button to open the Options dialog box. If you want to display the site name along with its IP address when tracing, turn on the Show DNS Names check box. You can change the number of packets sent with a ping, the time-out period, and other options.

Plotting with Ping Plotter

Another tracer program on the CD with this book is Ping Plotter, which you can download from http://www.nessoft.com/pingplotter.

To speed up the tracing, Ping Plotter actually sends out packets to the first 35 servers in the route all at the same time. Ping Plotter, with a trace to my ISP, is shown in Figure 37.4. It not only shows the IP address and name of each router, but it also shows the average and current times of the pings in a timeline graph next to the hop list, and in a graph of time along the bottom. The program continues to run, updating the times until you click Stop so you can monitor the speed of your connection over a period of time.

FIGURE 37.4   **PingPlotter**

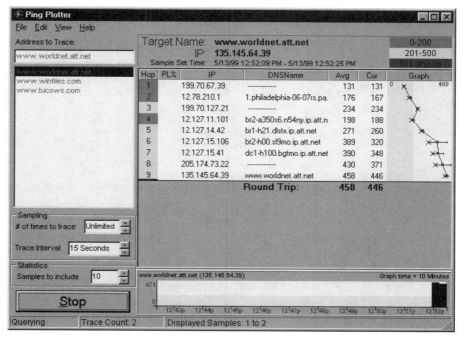

You can customize what appears on the timeline chart, adding the minimum and maximum times, by right-clicking it and choosing options from this menu:

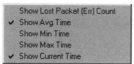

You can also right-click the chart at the bottom of the window to select other time periods, ranging from 1 minute to 24 hours.

Graphing with Neotrace

For the most graphic picture of the Web, run Neotrace. Version 1.22 of this program shows the route traveled using icons to indicate the type of site at each spot. If the destination of a particular path is a site in Germany, a German flag is used to denote the type of site or its location.

You can download Neotrace from `http://www.neoworx.com`. Start the program, type the IP or name of the site in the Host to Trace box and then click the Trace button in the toolbar along the left of the window.

A newer version of Neotrace is being developed that shows the route on a map. When you install this version, you specify your ZIP code or your longitude and latitude. The program gives you the option of displaying the route as a map, as icons, in a text list, or as a line graph.

Choices and More Choices

If you want to try some other programs that offer ping and trace route features, try some of these:

PROGRAM	DOWNLOAD SITE
DeEnesse	`http://www.cyberspacehq.com/deenesse`
Net Demon	`http://www.netdemon.net`
Netscan Tools	`http://www.nwpsw.com`
Network Toolbox	`http://www.jriver.com/products/networktoolbox.html`
Sam Spade	`http://www.blighty.com/products/spade`
Spike	`http://radsoft.net`
Cyberkit	`http://www.ping.be/cyberkit`

38 Busting Those Ads

You're looking at Tripod.com or some other site, and a second window pops up on your screen with an advertising message. You click its close button to remove it, but before you blink another pops up in its place. They appear almost as fast as you can close them.

Kill Those Pop-Up Windows and Annoying Ads

So much of the stuff on the Internet is free because advertising supports it. You pay for those free Web sites by being subjected to windows that pop up with advertising. Pop-up windows are getting to be about everywhere, but you can strike back!

Here's What You Need

You'll need your Web browser and a free or inexpensive program you can get from the CD or download from the Internet.

Sites and Features

Internet advertising is probably here to stay, just as commercials on television. With a TV, you can turn down the sound, run to the kitchen for a snack, or change the channel. But what can you do if the pop-up windows and other Internet ads get to you?

Plenty!

There are programs that are designed to keep these annoying ads from annoying you.

KillAd

If you want to get rid of the pop-up windows while you're browsing, try KillAd. This program monitors your browser for extraneous windows and closes them. You'll find the program on the CD, or you can download it from `http://www.wplus.net/pp/fsc`.

KillAd places an icon on your system tray. Double-click the icon to toggle the function on and off. It is off when the icon appears dimmed. When turned on, each time a pop-up appears, it quickly disappears—if you blink you'll miss it altogether. You can also hold down the CTRL key to temporarily disable the program. Right-click the icon for this menu:

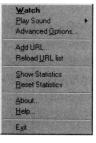

Select Watch to toggle the program on and off. Use the Play Sound option to control the sound played when a pop-up window is closed.

The default action that KillAd takes on windows depends on its settings. To see how the program is setup, and to customize it, select Advanced Options from the shortcut menu. You'll see the dialog box in Figure 38.1.

FIGURE 38.1 KillAd options

When the Hide option is not checked, pop-up windows are moved to the background, not closed. Enable Hide to completely remove the windows from your screen and from the Windows Taskbar.

The Wait for Caption Change option tells KillAd not to close the window until its title bar is complete.

Turn off the Kill Listed Popups Only option if you only want to close windows maintained in the list. If you turn off this option, KillAd considers a pop-up to be any browser window that opens in addition to the main browser window. Turning off this option may cause problems if you're using links that are supposed to open a second or third window.

To change the list of sites click Edit List. A Notepad window appears in which you can delete, edit, or add sites.

The Skip Maximized Browser Windows option is useful when you do not want to close windows to linked sites. If you are running with your browser maximized and it opens another window, this window will also be maximized. Choosing the Skip Maximized Browser Windows option prevents

KillAd from automatically closing the new maximized window that appears.

When a pop-up window appears, it is often given the keyboard focus. This means that any keys you press affect the pop-up window, not the original window you were viewing when the pop-up appeared. Use the options in the Restore Focus section to prevent this. When set at Online (once) the focus is restored to your original window as soon as the pop-up appeared. When set at Offline (always), the focus is restored each time the pop-up tries to take it.

The Enabled Browsers section determines which Web browsers the program monitors. The Pre-kill Extra Delay option lets you delay the closing of a pop-up window. Increase this setting if KillAd causes errors.

Rather than edit the URL list from the Advanced Options box, you can add a pop-up to the list by dragging it. When the pop-up appears the first time, right-click the icon and choose Add URL to see this dialog box:

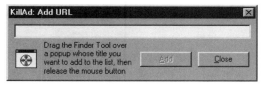

Drag the Finder Tool to the pop-up window, release the mouse button and click Add.

To quickly see how many ads the program saved you from watching, point to the icon in the system tray. A box appears showing the number of windows killed, ignored, and being watched. For more information, choose Show Statistics from the shortcut menu to see a box such as this:

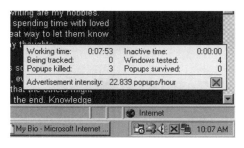

This box reports the amount of time you've had the program running and inactive, as well as the number of pop-ups per hour for your Internet session.

PointCast Adbuster

If you use PointCast to get on-screen news, try PointCast Adbuster. This program blocks out the ads in the upper-right corner of the PointCast window. You'll find the program on the CD with this book, and you can download it from `http://www.deyoung.net/joel/software/pcnbust/index.html`.

Install the program, then go to the folder where you placed it and run either Bust32 (for Windows 95/98/NT) or Bust16 (for Windows 3.1). The ad window in PointCast will now appear as a solid block of gray—not very pretty but not distracting.

To stop the program and start the ads, right-click its icon on the system tray and select Exit from the shortcut menu.

39 Share Your Phone Line

If your computers are networked, more than one person in the house can use the phone line to surf the Internet on the same Internet account with only one modem. The software may even be free depending on your version of Windows.

Don't Wait Till the Line Is Free

Just consider the benefits. With one phone line and one modem, everyone on your home network can access the Internet at the same time, browse different locations, download files, and send and receive e-mail. You don't need a second phone line or a second ISP account.

Here's What You Need

You'll need at least one phone line, one Internet account, and two or more networked computers. The network can be a peer-to-peer network using just Windows 95/98. If you have Windows 98 Second Edition, the software for sharing a phone line and modem is built-in. If you have an earlier version, you can get inexpensive software for modem sharing—there are even two on the CD with this book.

Sites and Features

To share a phone line and modem you have to be networked, which in itself involves some money. But network "starter kits" that let you connect two computers cost less than just one month of a second phone line and second Internet account. So once you are networked, you get to enjoy the benefit of sharing a phone and modem all year around.

The computer that contains the modem that you'll be sharing is called the *host*. The other computers on the network that will be using that modem are called the *clients*.

Now in addition to being networked, to share a modem you need the following things:

◆ You need to set up something called TCP/IP on your computer, but it is included with Windows.

◆ You need Internet sharing software, which is included in Windows 98 Second Edition.

◆ You need to install the software and make some minor adjustments to your Internet browser.

Setting Up the Host Computer

If you are networked, chances are TCP/IP is already on your computer. So let's start by checking to make sure it is there.

1. Select Start ➤ Settings ➤ Control Panel ➤ Network, and Configuration tab, if it is not already displayed.

2. If you see a listing in the list box for TCP/IP followed by the name of your network card, click Cancel. Otherwise, install TCP\IP by following these steps.

   1. Click Add, then select Protocol in the box that appears.

   2. Click Add in that dialog box. You'll see a list of hardware manufacturers on the left and protocols on the right.

   3. Choose Microsoft from the list on the left, and choose TCP/IP from the list on the right.

   4. Click OK twice, and then select Yes to restart your computer.

Next, if you have Windows 98 Second Edition, you can set up Internet sharing without any additional software. You do have to install Internet

Connection Sharing, however, because it is not installed automatically with Windows 98. Just follow these steps on the *host* computer. (You do not have to install Internet Connection Sharing on the client computers.)

1. Insert the Windows 98 Second Edition CD in your CD drive.

2. Select Start ➤ Settings ➤ Control Panel ➤ Add/Remove Programs in the Windows Control Panel and click the Windows Setup tab.

3. Select Internet Tools and then click the Details button to see a list of the items in the Internet Tools category.

4. In the Components box, turn on the Internet Connection Sharing check box, and then click OK twice. Windows installs the feature and then begins the Internet Connection Sharing Wizard.

5. Read and follow the instructions in the Wizard dialog boxes, clicking Next after each. At one point, you'll be asked to insert a disk in your floppy disk drive so Windows can create a program to configure the client computers for sharing.

6. Click Finish at the final Wizard dialog box, and then select Yes to restart your computer.

Setting Up Client Computers

That's all you'll need to do to the host computer. The next steps involve the clients. You should set up TCP\IP on each of the clients so they get their IP address automatically.

Follow these steps on each of the client computers.

1. Select Start ➤ Settings ➤ Control Panel ➤ Network.

2. Select the TCP/IP listing for your network card and click the Properties button.

3. Click the IP Address tab and select the option Obtain an IP Address Automatically.

4. Click the WINS Configuration tab, and confirm that the Use DHCP for WINS Resolution option is selected.

5. Click the Gateway tab, and confirm that the Installed Gateways list is empty.

6. Click the DNS Configuration tab, and select the Disable DNS option.

7. Click OK three times, and then select Yes to restart your computer.

The client computers are now set up for TCP/IP. The final step is to set their Internet browsers to connect over the network rather than dialing in. That's the purpose of the floppy disk you made on the host computer with Internet Connection Sharing.

1. Start the host computer and use it to connect to the Internet.

2. Insert the disk into the floppy drive and run the program `Icsclset` `.exe` on that disk to start the Browser Connection Setup Wizard.

3. Click Next until the last Wizard box appears and then click Finish.

You're now ready. As long as the host computer is turned on, any of the client computers on the network can connect to the Internet. If the host is already connected, the other computers just connect without having to dial in. If the host is not connected to the Internet, a client computer will actually dial in through the modem on the host to initiate the network's connection.

WinGate and RideWay

You can still share a phone line and modem if you do not have Windows 98 Second Edition. There are lots of programs, most of them are shareware, which can provide the same features as Microsoft's Internet Connection Sharing feature. The CD with this book includes two such programs, WinGate and Rideway.

You install WinGate on all of the computers on the network. The first dialog box of the installation program asks if you are setting up a WinGate Server (another name for a host) or a WinGate Internet Client. Choose the WinGate Server option on the computer you want to use as the host, and choose the Client option on the other computers.

The version of WinGate on the CD is a 30-day trial version for use by up to six computers at one time. When you install the program, you'll be asked for a license name and license key.

For the license name, enter Sybex. Enter it exactly as spelled, with the uppercase S, and remaining letters lowercase.

For the license key, enter the following exactly as it is shown:

AA6285939E998D1AA35A2B66

For more information about using WinGate, check out the program's help system, or go to `http://www.wingate.com` on the Internet.

To use the RideWay program, install it only on the computer you're using as the server, making a note of the server's IP address. On the client computers, you need to go to the Control Panel, open Network, and then double-click the listing for TCP/IP followed by your network card. On the DNS Configuration tab of the dialog box, enter the IP address of the server at the DNS Server Search Order text box. Finally, you have to set up your Web browser to access the Internet through the network. You'll find detailed instructions for doing this with the RideWay program, or at `http://www.itserv.com`.

Web Sites, Free or Easy

So far, you've been dealing with Web sites as an observer. Now it is time to be more of an active participant. In this chapter, you'll learn how to work with Web sites on a different level. You'll learn how to get files from Web sites, find out who owns a site, and get free Web sites for yourself. You'll also learn how to store files in those free Web sites and how to sign up for your own personal domain—http://www.you.com!

40   Grab Web Site Files

Ever see a neat graphic or hear a sound file when viewing a Web site? You can download these graphics, sounds, and individual files from Web sites; it is as easy as browsing.

View and Download the Contents of Web Sites

You've already learned that you can download entire Web sites for offline viewing. Sometimes, however, you're not interesting in the entire site; instead you are just interested in a graphic file, sound, or other file that's on the site. Rather than bringing over the entire site for offline browsing, you can identify the individual components that make up a Web site and get what you need.

Here's What You Need

The only things you will need are your Web browser and a program that you'll find on the CD or download from the Internet.

Sites and Features

Being able to grab selected files from a Web site means you can build up a great library of graphics, sounds, and other files that you find interesting. We'll take a look at two programs that help you do this, both of which you'll find on the CD with this book: Link Explorer and WebLeech. Both of these programs give you a much different view of a Web site than your browser. Rather than displaying the page as a graphic, they show the objects that are linked to the page.

As with offline browsing, you can select the number of levels of linked objects to display. You can view just the links on the site's home page, or the objects that are contained on the linked pages. You can then download any object that you see listed by either clicking it or dragging it onto your desktop. Remember, most of the files you'll find on Web sites are the property of the site owners. While you can use programs to download files, you cannot use the files commercially yourself. Get permission if you want to reproduce or otherwise use a file from a Web site.

Using Link Explorer

Link Explorer lets you view Web sites in a Window's Explorer type interface. You can find this product on the CD, or you can download it from `http://www.lightman.com/linkexplorer`.

Using Link Explorer, you can begin downloading files from a site. While it is downloading, you can continue browsing other locations. You can also schedule a file to be downloaded at a specific time. Here's how:

1. Start Link Explorer after you install it.

2. Type the Web address of the site you want to explore and press Enter. You could also use your Web browser to locate the page and then copy and paste its address into Link Explorer. The linked objects of the site will be listed on the right of the Link Explorer window, and the folders on your computer will be listed on the left.

3. Use the folder list on the left as you would Windows Explorer. Open the folder where you'd like to place the objects you'll copy from the site.

4. Drag a file from the right side of the window to the open folder on the left. You can also click the Download button in the toolbar, and then choose a location in the dialog box that appears. The evaluation version of Link Explorer on the CD will not allow you to drag-and-drop multiple files or load and save lists of links.

As the file is being downloaded, you can launch your browser and surf the Web. The icons in the status bar of the Link Explorer window display your progress. From left to right, the icons report

◆ Number of tasks remaining to be completed.

◆ Number of files you've scheduled to be downloaded at a later time.

◆ Number of completed downloads.

◆ Number of failed downloads.

Double-click an icon to see details of the tasks and downloads.

NOTE A download may fail if you try to get a file from a site that requires a user name and password. You'll find this most frequently when trying to download MP3 music files.

To schedule a download for a later time, follow these steps:

1. Click the file on the right, and then choose File ➤ Download Later.

2. In the dialog box that appears, select the location where you want to store the file, and then click Save.

3. Double-click any of the icons in the status bar.

4. Click the clock icon in the status bar to open the Tasks window.

5. Click the Timer button to open this dialog box.

6. Set the time and date and enable the Timer Active check box to start downloading.

7. Click OK.

On the other tabs of the Task Manager, you can change the order in which pending tasks are downloaded, delete tasks that are pending, open downloaded files, and retry those that failed. The Activity Log displays and reports the details of Link Explorer's actions, including why a download failed.

The Easy Search button on the Link Explorer toolbar gives you access to a multimedia search engine for MP3 and other sound files.

Pull down the top list and choose the search engine you want to use. Enter a keyword or phrase to identify the music you're looking for and then click OK. Link Explorer will locate sites containing matching files, and display them on the right side. You can then attempt to download files by dragging them to a destination folder.

Using WebLeech

WebLeech is a similar program to Link Explorer, but it uses its own interface for viewing files. You can find WebLeech on the CD or download it from http://www.voodoo-software.com.

When you run WebLeech, you'll see a listing of the files on the Web site on the right, and your hard disk on the left. To download a file, select it in the list on the right, and then click the Copy button.

There is a also a new version of the program, called WebLeech 2, that has an Explorer-like interface similar to Link Explorer. Check out WebLeech 2 at the voodoo-software site.

41 Who Owns That Web Site?

Most Web sites have a link to send e-mail to the sponsor or Webmaster, but some don't. If you want to know who's responsible for a Web site—either because you love it or hate it—find out who is in charge.

Find Out Who Runs What

All Web site domain names (the xxxx.com moniker) must be registered with a company called InterNIC. The registration includes the name and address of the organization holding the domain, a phone number, and sometimes the names of the responsible individuals.

Here's What You Need

You'll need your browser, your ISP, and some free or inexpensive software from the CD in this book or downloaded from the Internet.

Sites and Features

InterNIC has thoughtfully provided a function called Whois that will report the basic registration information if you give it the domain name.

To access Whois, you need to navigate to a Web site that offers free domain name lookup, or you will need to use a free or shareware program, many of which can be downloaded on the Internet or can be found on the accompanying CD with this book. Whois is very simple to use—just type the domain name and let it do its thing.

Two sites on the net that offer domain name lookup are `http://www.icom.com/dns.html`, and `http://www.domainvalet.com/register`. At sites like these, enter the domain name you are looking for, choose the domain type, and then click Check Name. The domain will be looked up and you'll see the name, address, phone number, and other information about the registered owner of the domain.

There are also plenty of programs that you can get that offer the Whois feature. For example, you can download a Whois program from `http://www.cix.co.uk/~net-services`. Many general dial-up networking utility programs also contain the Whois function. This includes ConnectPal, a program included on the accompanying CD. This program is covered in more detail in Section 33.

To use the downloaded program, just type the domain name in the Host text box and click Go. Enter the domain name without the "www" prefix— just `Microsoft.com` or `Corel.com` will work. The program dials into your ISP if you are not already online, connects to InterNIC, and reports the registered owner of the domain.

42 Free Web Sites

This is one of the best bargains of all time! More and more people are getting their own sites on the Web, so why not you? Most ISPs offer Web sites to their members, but they can be difficult to set up and use. With free Web sites, you don't even need an ISP, just access to the Internet.

Make Your Web Presence Known

Just think of it. For free, you'll have a place on the Internet to make your opinions known, and you'll also be able to share information with friends, relatives, and complete strangers. You can advertise a product, ask for information, or just have a place to learn about Web site design. What a bargain.

Here's What You Need

All you will need is access to the Internet. You can set up your own Web site from the local library or anyplace where you can connect to the Web.

Sites and Features

First of all, what distinguishes these free Web sites from the ones you can create with an ISP?

ISP	FREE
You must be a paying member.	You don't pay a thing.
You can have sophisticated, multiple page sites.	You may be limited to a set number of pages.
You can build your Web site using any Web-creation software.	You may have to use the site's program to create your Web page.
There won't be any advertisements on your site unless you put them there.	There may be advertisements on your site that you didn't put there.

Given those distinctions, free Web sites are great, even if you already have a site through your ISP. You can use these free sites for your children, or for temporary information that you want to make available. You can put personal information on the site that you would not place in your business site, or vice versa. And while some of the free sites limit you to just a few pages using their own special software, others are just as good—if not better—than most ISPs.

Just to emphasize a point, you can create a free Web site even if you do not have an Internet account. You just need access to the Internet. Once you create the site, it exists on the service's computer. So anyone with an Internet access can then access it. What if they want to send you e-mail? No trouble—just get a free e-mail account.

There are plenty of places where you can create a free Web site. I will discuss three sites in this section, but there are at least a thousand more, so don't feel limited to these.

Some serve a special geographic area, such as http://www.chez.com, which limits its members to those in France. Others are aimed at certain themes or groups. The site http://www.henterprises.com/webucat, for example, is devoted to school home pages. For a list of free Web site offers around the world, lookup http://uk.zarcrom.com/freehome.html.

Because some of these sites require you to use their own software, you are also limited to their design choices. Therefore, you cannot use a program such as Front Page and then upload the site. There are exceptions, however—some of the sites just give you a block of space and you're on your own. We'll look at these types of sites later.

If you create a free Web site using any service, make sure you record the site address and your password, along with any other registration information you enter.

Treeway.com

This is a great site because you can use the site for just about anything. You design up to eight pages using interactive forms on-screen. You don't have to know anything about HTML or uploading. You can also get a free e-mail account.

Navigate to `http://www.treeway.com` to see the site shown in Figure 42.1, and then click the Free Web site graphic. You'll be taken though the process of registering as a Treeway.com member and getting a Treeway.com e-mail address.

FIGURE 42.1   **Treeway.com offers free Web sites**

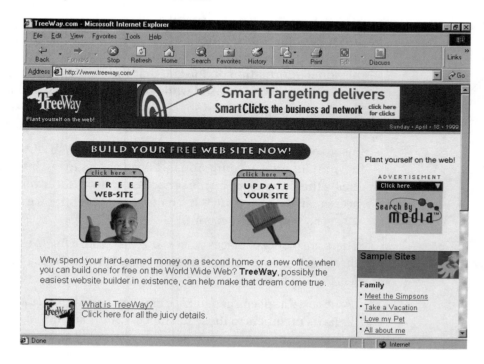

Once you sign in, you're taken through a series of screens in which you design your Web site by adding text and selecting design elements and themes. Each theme consists of a series of graphics that appear on your site. You can also choose an overall layout.

You can easily add and delete pages, change the layout, add graphics and text. Treeway.com doesn't clutter up your site with any advertisements, except for one small line at the bottom pointing to the Treeway.com home page, as shown in Figure 42.2. That's a small price to pay for the free service. The address of your site is `http://members.treeway.com/your-member-name`.

FIGURE 42.2   **Free home page on Treeway.com**

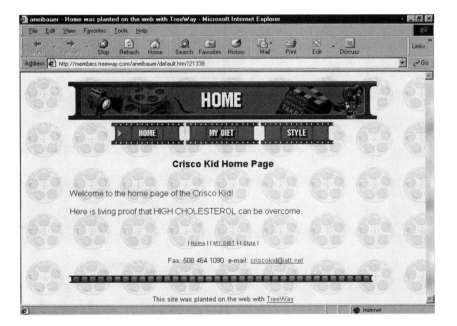

MyFamily.com

This service is aimed at family-oriented sites, hence its name! All of the sites created through it use a standard format; you add your own information. Navigate to `http://www.myfamily.com` and click the link *Start a family web site.* You'll be taken through several screens in which you register as the administrator of the site and enter a site name.

The focus of MyFamily.com is to offer a meeting place for family members and family information. You invite family members to join the site, give them permission to view it, add information, and upload files and pictures that they want to share with other family members. A typical site under construction is shown in Figure 42.3. Sites are private—your invited family members must log on to it.

FIGURE 42.3   Site under construction at MyFamily.com

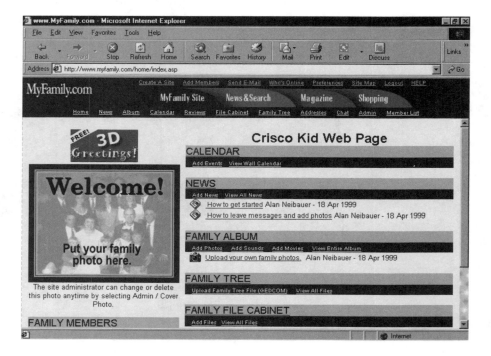

Tripod

If you want a little more freedom in creating a Web page, try http://www .tripod.com. Tripod gives you 11 megabytes of free storage space, which is larger than many ISPs give paying members. It also allows you to create pages online using their software, or upload Web pages you create using any Web creation software.

When you get to Tripod, click Sign Up. You'll be taken through a number of screens in which you enter your name and e-mail address, and select a member name and password.

Tripod offers three basic options for creating sites:

Easy Step-by-Step Building   Lets you create a complete site by selecting options and entering text.

Make some HTML Magic   Allows you to enter the HTML code that creates a page.

Edit & Update With Ease   Lets you modify a site and upload pages from your computer. You can also upload pages using an FTP program.

If you're a beginner, you can use the Easy Step-by-Step Building option to create some rather sophisticated pages. In fact, the option gives you the following choices:

◆ **Quickstart**   Goes step-by-step through creating a basic Website.

◆ **Quicktopic**   Lets you design a site based on its topic.

◆ **Quickdesign**   Lets you create a site by selecting design elements.

Tripod is a very community-oriented site. It offers additional features and provided forums where members can share information and experiences. It does require that you update, change, or add to your site every 30 days to keep it current. If you fail to update your site, Tripod retains the option to close it down, but you can reregister your site any time.

One drawback is that while Tripod offers a powerful range of features and plenty of storage space, it does show a pop-up ad and some advertising at the top of your site. This may be a drawback, because it makes your site look like a commercial one.

43 Storing and Sharing Documents

Most ISPs make it easy to get a basic Web site. But once you've added the standard "Here's My Homepage and Welcome To It" page then what? You're now ready for more interesting things.

So You Have a Web Site. Now What?

Even if you don't want a Web site at all, you can use your space to store and share documents of all types. Just think of free Web sites as a little extra disk space that you can access from anywhere on Earth.

Here's What You Need

You need to have a Web site on your ISP's server established. You may also need some basic information to get started.

First, find out from your ISP if you can upload information directly using File Transfer Protocol (FTP). If not, you're stuck using their own programs for creating your Web site. If they do let you use FTP, ask them for the following information: host name or IP address for using FTP, your user ID, your password, and the initial directory, if you need it.

The host name or IP address refers to a specific computer at the service provider's site. It is not the address of your ISP's home page. It may be the IP address of the computer where your actual Web site is stored, or a general location where all of the ISP member sites are kept (such as upload.att.net, or something like that).

The User ID and password may be the same as the ones you use to log on or the one you use to send and receive e-mail. It is also possible that a special ID and password are assigned specifically for Web site management.

The initial directory is used when you are uploading to a general ISP site, because it identifies your specific area. For example, with AT&T Worldnet, every user accesses their home page starting with the site upload.att.net. The initial directory, however, is their user name, which tells AT&T where to put the files when they are uploaded.

Sites and Features

Most ISPs help you create a simple Web page by taking you through a series of menus and dialog boxes. The information that you enter and select is used to create the Web site.

You may have some other program that you'd like to use to create a Web page, such as Microsoft Front Page (that comes with Microsoft Office) or Trellix (that comes with WordPerfect Office). Perhaps you'd rather create a Web site using one of those programs rather than the step-by-step method provided by the ISP.

Or, maybe you don't want a Web site at all! Should all that free Web site space go to waste? Not at all. You can use your Web site—whether provided by an ISP or one of the free Web sites offered by other companies—for many other purposes:

◆ Store pictures that you want to show friends or relatives. Rather than e-mail your picture to everyone on your list, you can place it on your

Web site. This way, all of your friends who have access to the Internet can see the picture.

◆ Hold documents that you want to share with others. Do you have a document that you want to send to someone else? Rather than e-mail it, put it on your Web site so others can download it when they are ready.

◆ Distribute software. Written an interesting computer program? Found a freeway program that you'd like to share? You can put either on your Web site as well.

◆ Backup files for safekeeping. You know that very important report that you've been writing? In addition to saving it on a floppy for safekeeping, store a copy on your Web site. Then, even if a spaceship flies over your house and zaps every disk in the place, you are still protected.

◆ Make a file accessible from any location. Do you work at home and in the office? While on the road and on vacation? If you have Internet access at every location, don't bother carrying around a bunch of floppies. Store your working documents on your Web site and just download them from there when needed.

The trick to all of these features is *uploading*. Uploading means to copy files from your hard disk to your Web site. You may be able to upload files using online programs provided by your ISP. But that means getting online and going through a series of menus to make it happen. If your ISP allows you to send via FTP, then you're in luck, because there's plenty of free and inexpensive software to help you.

With an FTP program, you are connected to two computers at once—yours (called the local computer) and your ISP's (called the remote computer)—and you can move files between them in either direction. Moving a file from your computer to the ISP's is called uploading. Moving a file from the ISP's computer to your own is called downloading.

First of all, Windows comes with an FTP program that doesn't cost you an extra dime. There is a price to pay, of course. It is not the easiest program to use because it runs strictly from the DOS command prompt. See DOS isn't really dead at all, just dormant.

The exact sequence for using FTP depends on your ISP but it could go something like this:

1. Click Start ➤ Programs ➤ MS-DOS Prompt.

2. Type **FTP**, a space, and then the address of the site.

3. Press Enter. Windows will dial into your ISP. If it does not, try connecting to the Internet first, and then go to the MS-DOS prompt and run FTP.

4. At the prompt, enter your user name and press Enter.

5. At the prompt, enter your password and press Enter.

6. Type **binary** to transfer non-text files, and press Enter.

7. Type **Interactive Mode Off**, to turn off the interactive mode.

8. Type **CD**, a space, and the name of the folder where you want to add the files, and press Enter.

9. Type **put**, followed by the path and name of the file, and press Enter.

10. Type **bye** and press Enter when you want to quit the FTP program.

It is a lot of typing, and there are plenty of chances to screw up and enter the wrong command. It actually isn't that difficult as long as you know the routine. But if you're not interested in the routine, then there's a perfect solution. Get yourself a free or inexpensive FTP program. Most of the programs are available for downloading and use a graphic interface. That means you upload files by clicking or dragging rather than by using a long series of DOS commands.

There are literally hundreds of FTP programs out there. Here are just a few:

◆ FTP Voyager, which you can get from `http://www.deerfield.com`.

◆ FTP Explorer listed with `http://www.download.com`.

◆ FTP Commander at `http://www.vista.ru`.

◆ Crystal FTP and CuteFTP at `http://www.download.com`.

Using WS_FTP

We'll take a close look at a great program called WS_FTP. The program comes in two versions, standard and Pro. The standard program is free if you use it non-commercially, and it can be downloaded from `http://www` `.ipswitch.com`. The Pro version is not free, but it has lots of extra features, including two interfaces and the ability to synchronize sites. The limited time trial version WS_FTP PRO is available on the CD.

WS_FTP gives you a visual interface for uploading programs, so you don't have to worry about DOS commands. You can even rename, delete, and copy files on your Web site, just as easily as if they were on your own hard disk. It's like working remotely on your ISP's computer.

Figure 43.1 shows the opening dialog box of WS_FTP Pro. The folders represent popular sites for downloading software and other information.

FIGURE 43.1 Select a site in WS_FTP Pro.

Just double-click the site you want to go to. You'll learn later how to download files from a site.

Since we're interested in uploading programs for now, your first task it to create a listing for your Web page. Here's how.

1. Click the folder where you want to store your connection (usually My Sites).

2. Click New in the WS_FTP Sites box to open the New Site/Folder dialog box.

3. Type a name for the site—something like My Site at isp.com is fine—and then click Next.

4. In the box that appears, type the host name or IP address of the upload site—you'll need to get this from your ISP— then click Next.

5. In the box that appears, enter your User ID, your password, and enable the Save Password option.

6. Click Finish. Your FTP site will now be added to the list in the WS_FTP Sites box.

If you need to specify an initial directory, however, you have to do so before connecting to the site. Click the site name in the list and then on the Properties button. In the dialog box that appears, click the Startup tab to see the options in Figure 43.2. In the Remote Site Folder text box, type your user name or folder name, then click OK.

FIGURE 43.2 Setting the initial remote directory

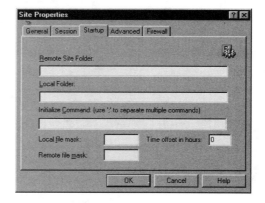

Now, to connect to your site, select the site name and click OK. WS_FTP will connect to the Internet through your ISP and log on to your Web site for access. You'll see a list of the files on your site in the box on the right, as in Figure 43.3. The list on the left shows the files on the current folder of your computer.

FIGURE 43.3 Access a site with WS_FTP

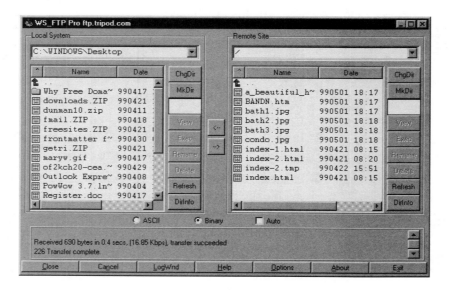

To upload files, you have to list them on the left. Click ChgDir, enter the path where the files are stored on your disk, and then click OK. On the list on the left, click a file, and then hold down the CTRL key and click any other files that you want to move to the Web site. Finally, click the button that has the icon of a right-pointing arrow to copy the files to your site. As the files are transferred, you'll see a status report in the bottom window and a progress box on the screen. When the files are uploaded, click Close and then Exit.

WARNING Always click Close before exiting and wait until the file list on the right is empty.

Downloading Files by FTP You can use programs such as WS_FTP to download as well as upload files. Using the classic interface, click the file you want to download on the right of the screen, and then click the button that has the icon of a left pointing arrow. Using the Explorer interface, just drag the file onto your desktop or into a folder on your disk.

Accessing Web Site Files If you want to share a photo by posting it on a Web site, just give people the site address. For example, if your site is `http://members.myISP.com/~myname`, and the picture is `party.jpg`, anyone can see the picture by pointing their browser at `http://members.myISP .com/~myname/party.jpg`.

With documents, programs, zip files, or any other file that the browser cannot display automatically, the browser will display the familiar box asking if you want to open or save the file. Just click Save and then OK to download the file to your computer.

When you place a file on the Internet, remember that it is accessible to anyone who can get to that address. If you want to keep a file private, you can password protect it in a couple of ways.

◆ Some ISPs let you password protect your site. This means you can designate a password that must be entered before the site can be seen.

◆ You can use a program such as WinZip to compress the file with a password. A person must have the password to unzip the file.

44 Get Your Own Domain

You can join the ranks of the world's largest companies and educational institutions by having your own name on the Internet.

Sign Up As *YOU.COM*

Having your own domain on the Internet is easy and not that expensive to achieve. While it costs more than a free Web site, to be sure, your own domain will really establish your presence on the Internet.

Here's What You Need

You'll need access to the Web and at least $70.00. The $70.00 registers your domain name with an organization called the Internet Network Information Center (InterNIC) for two years—it costs $35.00 a year after that. If you want to actually have a Web site at your own domain, you'll need to pay a monthly Web hosting fee.

NOTE The United States government has contracted with a company called Network Solutions Inc. to control InterNIC.

Registering your own domain just means reserving the name (me.com, for example) so no one else can claim it. It does not actually put a Web site on the Internet. I was a little late in my own case, for example, and my cousin reserved http://www.neibauer.com before me, so I had to reserve http://www.neibauer.net.

When the Internet first started, having a domain meant that you had a computer called an Internet Server connected directly to the Internet. If you connect to the Internet through an ISP, then you're not directly connected, so in addition to registering your domain name, you have to find someone to either *park* or *host* your site.

Parking means that your domain name will be associated with an actual place on the Internet—an IP address—that is on someone else's Internet Server. When you park a domain name, the site will be empty except for a message or graphic reporting that there is nothing there. There are companies that will park your domain name for free.

Hosting your site means that you actually have space on the server's computer to place your Web page. This is rarely given away free. Most ISPs that give you a Web page and companies that offer free Web pages will not let you do it under your own domain name. So to actually use your site, you need to find a company that will host your site for a monthly charge. That's not a problem because there are plenty of them. Many of them will also handle the task of registering your domain name at the same time—you still have to pay the $70.00 fee, of course. Having your site hosted on someone else's server is called having a *virtual domain*.

Hosting fees range anywhere from about $5.00 to thousands a month, depending on the amount of disk space and the services provided. Getting a small Web site for a few pages, for example, will certainly cost less than a large corporate Web site. But in addition to the amount of space, the rates vary according to the Web site features you want to use. It will cost you more, for instance, if you want to sell your products online using a secure order entry system that accepts credit card sales. The rates also vary according to the number of e-mail addresses available at the site.

NOTE In addition to the monthly hosting charge, you'll still need to belong to an ISP, have access to the Internet one way or the other, or pay someone to manage your site for you.

Sites and Features

If you just want to reserve your domain name rather than actually have a site, you can find companies that will help you process the registration form and park the site on their server. For example, check out `http://www.domainvalet.com/index.html`.

DomainValet will register your domain name for you and park your site for no charge beyond the $70.00 InterNIC registration fee. Why do they do it for you? They hope that you decide to have them host your site at a later time. If you choose another host, you can transfer your domain name to it.

If you actually want to have a Web page on the site, then you need to have it hosted. There are literally thousands of Web hosting sites.

The first place to start looking for a hosting company is with your ISP. Some ISPs offer the service for an additional monthly charge. If yours doesn't, or you think they charge too much, then search the Internet for the terms "website hosting" or "web hosting."

N O T E   You can get Web hosting for free from http://www.click2site.com, but your site will carry some banner advertising.

Getting Your Own Domain

To show how easy it is to get your own domain, we'll use the hosting service http://www.11net.com as an example. This Web hosting service offers low monthly rates and will handle the chore of registering your own domain name. Signing up takes less than five minutes, and you don't even need a charge card! In fact, you'll find my own domain, http://www.neibauer.net, hosted by 11Net.com.

If you want to have your own Internet domain hosted by 11Net.com, just follow these steps.

1. Connect to the Internet and navigate http://to www.11net.com. As you can see, hosting starts at $6.99 per month.

2. Click the Sign Up icon to start the process on the form (see Figure 44.1). The company offers two levels of service. Plan 1 is $6.99 a month for 60MB of space and three e-mail accounts. Plan 2 is $14.99 a month with 100MB of space and 10 e-mail accounts. With Plan 2, you can also get detailed statistics about traffic to your site and you can use a secure method of getting information, such as charge card numbers if you sell a product.

N O T E   Having your own CGI-BIN (Common Gateway Interface Binary) means that you can run custom programs, or *scripts*, that you maintain on the Web server.

3. On the sign-up form, select either Plan 1 or Plan 2, and then scroll the page down to continue with the form.

FIGURE 44.1   11Net.com's sign up form

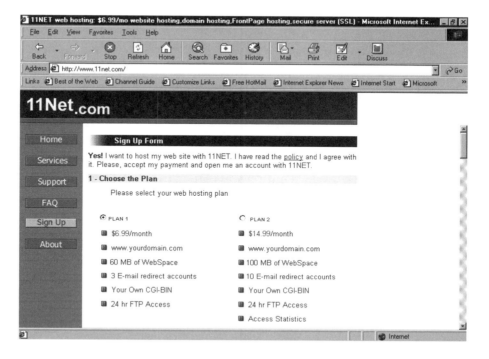

4. Choose if you want Front Page support. Front Page is a popular program from Microsoft that lets you create Web sites. If your hosting company supports Front Page, you can keep your site up-to-date automatically from within the Front Page program. If your site does not support Front Page, you have to transfer files to it using FTP. Some companies charge extra for Front Page support—11Net.com doesn't.

5. Select the type of URL. You can sign up for a virtual domain (http:// www.yourname.com) or to have it hosted under 11Net.com (www.11net .com/yourname). You can either enter a new domain name you want to register, or transfer an existing domain to the 11Net.com server.

6. Click Check if the domain name is available to use Whois. This will confirm that the name you want is not currently registered.

7. Select a login name. You'll use this name to log on to the site to upload files, using either an FTP program or Front Page. The company will later assign you a password.

8. Enter your name and address to be used by 11Net.com for billing as well as your domain registration.

9. Select either a six-month or 12-month payment period. There's a $20.00 setup fee if you choose six months that is waived if you sign up for a year.

10. Choose to pay by charge card, check, or money order.

11. Specify how you heard about 11Net.com. (In the *Please Specify if Other* text box, type **Alan's Book.** Thanks!)

12. Enter any special instructions about your account.

13. Click Next. You'll see a summary of your answers to the sign-up form.

14. If there are any mistakes on the form, click your browser's Back or Previous button and correct them. Otherwise, click Submit.

Wait a few minutes and then check your e-mail. You'll soon get a notification that your payment to 11Net.com is due in 10 days. Send in your check or money order, or click the link in the e-mail that shows where you can pay by credit card.

You'll also get an e-mail explaining some important information about your hosting account along with your login password and a temporary URL to use until the domain registration is approved. Print a copy of the e-mail for your records.

When 11Net.com sends you its e-mail, it also sends your completed domain application to InterNIC. Within two weeks you'll be officially notified that your registration has been approved. Until then, you can start building your Web site at the temporary URL assigned by 11Net.com.

That's it. You're now on the Internet with your own domain!

E-Mail

Most hosting services offer e-mail accounts along with the Web site. If you register http://www.myname.com, you can have mail sent to me@myname.com.

Some hosts provide an actual e-mail server. Depending on the host, you can use a program such as Outlook Express or Eudora to send and receive e-mail through the server, or you can send and receive e-mail by connecting to their site on the Internet.

Other hosts offer e-mail forwarding. With 11Net.com, for instance, you get 3 or 10 e-mail addresses, depending on the plan you select. You use the 11Net.com form, shown in Figure 44.2, to create the e-mail accounts and designate where the mail is forwarded. Any e-mail received by your domain will automatically be forwarded to the address specified, unbeknownst to the sender.

FIGURE 44.2 Creating e-mail accounts in 11Net.com

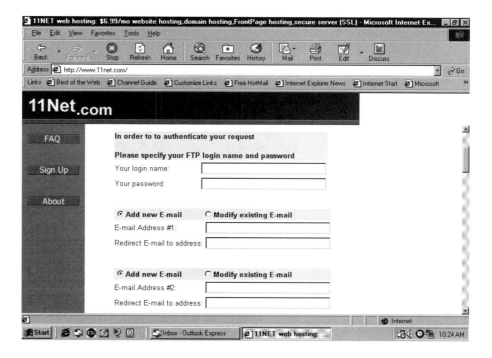

Putting Up Your Web Site

Now that you have your own domain, you have to upload your Web page to it. You can have as many pages and files on the site as will fit, but your initial page must have a special name, depending on the hosting company.

The file name is always some variation of either index.htm or index.html. Depending on the hosting company the name may be case-sensitive. If your host requires the file index.html, as does 11Net.com, you cannot name it Index.html because the case of each character does not match. With some hosts the case does not matter, so you could name yours INDEX.HTML, Index.HTML, or index.html. The extension also matters. If your host requires htm, do not use html.

When someone navigates to your site, they automatically see the index file that you uploaded to the site. If you just signed up for a domain and did not install a site of your own, there will be a standard index file placed there by the host. It will probably be some message that the site is under construction. You have to design and upload your own index file containing all of the files and graphics to your host site (remember to check and make sure you are using the right case).

There are plenty of ways to design a Web page. Programs such as Microsoft Word and Corel WordPerfect let you create a Web pages as easily as if you were writing and formatting a document. You can save the document in HTML format, and name it Index.htm or Index.html.

Other programs, such as Microsoft Front Page and Trellix, let you create Web sites of multiple pages linked together. You might already have some program that lets you create an HTML document, or, if you don't, you can find shareware programs all over the Internet.

Once you have the Web page or site created, you have to upload it to the host computer. You can do this using FTP or the Front Page program, if your host supports it.

In Section 43, *Storing and Sharing Documents*, you learned how to upload information to a free Web site using FTP. You use the same technique to upload pages to your own virtual domain.

Using WS_FTP, which comes on the accompanying CD, you can upload your site using your domain as the host name, and your login name and password.

NOTE Check with your host for the proper directory for your Web site files.

Counting Hits

You may want a *hit counter* on your page. This simply counts the number of times a Web page has been accessed.

If you are using Microsoft Front Page, and your host supports it, you can add a hit counter by just selecting Insert ➤ Component ➤ Hit Counter from the Front Page menu bar. Otherwise, you'll need to insert one or more lines of HTML instructions into your Web page.

The easiest way to create a hit counter is to ask your hosting company if they have a built-in counter program. If they do, they can give you the HTML line that you can insert into your page where you want the counter to appear.

With 11Net.com, for example, all you need to do is enter a line like this:
```
<img src="http://www2.11net.com/cgi-bin/count.cgi?test" align=
"absbottom">.
```

N O T E The www2 part of the command varies with the specific server you are assigned in 11Net.

This line of HTML accesses a hit counter maintained by 11Net.com, inserts the counter into your Web page, and keeps a running count of the number of times the page is accessed.

N O T E You can have a different hit counter on more than one page of your site to see how often specific pages are accessed. Just use a different name (in place of *test* in the sample) on each page.

If your host does not maintain a built-in hit counter, you can access free ones made available by other companies. Check out these sites for free counter programs:

◆ `http://www2.freestats.com`

◆ `http://counters.qpt.com`

◆ `http://www.fastcounter.com`

◆ `http://www.digits.com/create.html`

Plenty of Options

As I said, there are thousands of hosting services out there. In addition to 11Net.com, take a look at `http://www.hostingsolutions.net`.

N O T E There is also a company at `http://www.hostingsolutions.com` that offers plans starting at $9.95 for 10MB of space up to $59.95 for 100MB of space; this company will park your domain for $20.00 a year.

Hosting Solutions offers several levels of personal and business plans. Personal plans range from $9.95 per month for 5MB of space to $14.95 per month for 10MB. The plans include free domain registration—of course, you're still responsible for the $70.00 InterNIC fee.

Their business plans range from $19.95 to $49.95. The business plans provide additional storage space, maintain mailing lists, and feature business needs for online commerce.

All of the plans at Hosting Solutions also include a certain amount of network traffic and a number of e-mail accounts.

Network traffic measures the amount of activity on your site—the number of accesses and the amount of data that's moved in and out each month. The business plans provide for more traffic than the personal plans. Traffic beyond what is included in the plan incurs additional charges. The personal plans, for example, allow for 1GB or 3GB, while the business plans range from 5GB to 30GB per month. Additional traffic costs $1.00 per 100MB.

The POP mail accounts mean that you can check your mail using programs such as Outlook Express, from any computer that has Internet access. The number of accounts depends on the plan, from one account for personal plans up to 75 for the most costly business plan. Additional e-mail accounts cost $5.00 per month for every five accounts.

The Bottom Line

There are a lot of choices on the Internet for hosting your own domain, so take your time and shop around. Your choice should depend not only on price but also on the services offered. If you're creating a family Web site, for example, you may want a host that offers an e-mail account for each member of the family, either on an actual server or forwarded to your ISP.

You may not need some of the more sophisticated services that are typical in business accounts (such as security for online purchases and CGI scripts). Just make sure that the amount of space provided is sufficient for your purposes. Most personal sites can easily fit in 5MB of space, unless they include many high-resolution graphics and special effects.

So what's the final cost of having your own domain on the Internet? It is a minimum of $70.00 for two years if you create your own Web page and find a company that offers free hosting.

If you have to pay for hosting, you can find companies that charge $5.00 and up. The most typical hosting charge ranges from $15.00 to $25.00 per month, but you can do better if you shop around.

Based on a $15.00 monthly hosting charge and the InterNIC fees, your domain will cost $215.00 per year. If you pay $20.00 per month to your ISP, your total annual Internet bill is about $455.00. That's not that much to pay for a presence on the Internet equal to that of the Fortune 500 companies.

Buying Online

There are a lot of free things on the Internet, but there are a lot of good things to buy as well. You can find all sorts of items that can be delivered right to your door, and at great prices. The Internet is also a great place to sell things, whether you have a business or just want to clear out that old junk from the attic.

45 The World's Largest Bookstores

Without ever leaving your home, you can access the world's largest selection of books for sale. "So everybody already knows that," you say. But do you know that you can get hard to find out-of-print and antique books as well?

Order Any Type of Book Online

Remember that great book you had when you were a child? Do you collect books and paraphernalia about the Civil War or some other subject? Because of the global nature of the Internet, you can locate hard-to-find books on virtually every subject.

Here's What You Need

All you will need is access to the Internet and a credit card that hasn't expired or exceeded its limit.

Sites and Features

First, to buy current books, check out one of these sites:

- ◆ http://www.amazon.com
- ◆ http://www.fatbrain.com
- ◆ http://www.barnesandnoble.com
- ◆ http://www.borders.com

Each of these sites have an easy search function for finding the book you want, and each features current best sellers right on their home page. You can also try the home pages of most publishers for book and ordering information. You just might be able to purchase directly from the publisher at a discount.

Searching Many Stores with AddALL

Rather than search through the individual stores, you can search several at one time. By navigating to `http://www.addall.com`, for example, you can enter search criteria into a form and search 40 bookstores.

N O T E You can also use addALL to search for music and sign up for free, Web-based e-mail.

Here's how to use the form:

1. Pull down the Shipping Destination list, and choose the country or region where you want to send the book.

2. If shipping in the United States, select the state in the State list.

3. Choose the currency in which you want the prices displayed.

4. Pull down the Search By list, and select how you want to search the bookstores. The options are Title, ISBN, Author, and Keyword.

5. In the text box to the right of the Click to Find button, enter the search text—a title, ISBN number, author name, or keyword.

6. Click the Click to Find button.

You'll see a list of books meeting your search criteria. Click a book title to compare the pricing and availability at various online bookshops. To order the book, click Buy It to the right of your selected source.

To look for used, rare, and out-of-print books, click the *Search for Used Books* link that's below the `addall.com` form. In the form that appears, enter your search criteria, select the bookstores you want to search, and then click Find the Book. You'll get a listing of online sites, which have that book listed in their catalog, along with their asking price.

Searching with BookFinder.com and Bibliofind

The Web site at `http://www.bookfinder.com` also lets you search for new, used, rare, and out-of-print books using a similar form. At this site, you can also designate the binding (all, hardcover, or paperback), whether you want a first edition or a signed copy, and the price range. The results appear in a separate table for each online store.

Many of the search companies include http://www.bibliofind.com as one of their search sites for used and out-of-print books. You can also go to that site directly to look for books yourself. At bibliofind, you can maintain a personal "want list" of books you are looking for.

Bibliofind maintains a database of books in a large number of bookstores. The results of your search are displayed as a list of books, each proceeded with a check box.

Enable the check boxes next to each entry for books you want to order, or click the Seller's link to read more about the seller. Click the price of a book to display the price in many of the world's currencies. If there are more books than can be listed in one page, click the More Titles button at the bottom of the list.

If the book you are looking for is not listed, you can scroll to the end to display the Personal Want List form. Enter information about a book you're looking for, and click the Place on Want List button. The list is available to Bibliofind's member stores, and you'll be notified if the book is located.

Once you've enabled the boxes for the books you want to purchase, click the button labeled Add to Shopping Basket at the bottom of the list. You'll see a screen summarizing your order. Click the button labeled Place Order to enter your address, charge information, and process the order. At this screen, you'll also have a chance to empty your shopping basket if you change your mind.

46 Buying at Internet Auctions

Auctions such as eBay and Amazon can give you the same thrill as a real live auction house, but from the comfort of your home or office. The auction at eBay, for example, may have over 1.5 million items up for grab at any one time. You'll find something for every collection, both old and new merchandise, and some real bargains.

Making Sure You Win

The trick to getting what you want is to win the bid at a price you think is fair, and then actually get what you paid for. Some folks get carried away with the spirit of competition and end up paying more than they want—and often more than the object is worth.

Here's What You Need

All you will need to get started is access to the Internet and an e-mail address. Of course, when you start bidding, you will also need to dig for your checkbook.

Sites and Features

There are plenty of online auctions, but the granddaddy of them all is at http://www.ebay.com. Amazon and other companies have their own auctions, but eBay seems to get the most number and variety of items for sale.

If you're not familiar with online auctions, here's how they work. People with stuff to sell, and people who want to buy things, register with the auction by giving their e-mail address, and usually their name, and mailing address. Registration is free. The sellers list items for sale. The listing includes a short description of the item, a minimum bid, and often a photograph of the item for sale. The description also states who pays the shipping charges—usually the buyer. The seller pays a small listing fee, usually under a dollar.

The auction is then started for the item for a set number of days—7 to 10 is about the average. Some auctions even let the seller select the number of days.

People who may want to buy the item leave a bid on it by filling out a form. You can check back regularly to see how the auction is going, and who has the current high bid.

Most auctions send a daily e-mail to the seller with the current high bids on their items. The buyer may be notified if they are outbid on an item, giving them a chance to submit a higher bid.

EBay and other auctions have *proxy bidding*. This means that you can leave the highest amount that you are willing to pay for the item. The auction house will post your bid as either the minimum bid or one dollar above the current winner. If someone bids higher than you, it raises your bid but not above the maximum that you set.

For example, suppose you see an antique that you are interested in. It has a $10.00 minimum bid and you can leave a maximum offer of $20.00. If no one else has yet bid on the item, you're bid is recorded for just $10.00. If someone else has already bid at $10.00, your offer is shown as $11.00.

Each time someone outbids you, the auction raises your bid to make it the highest until it reaches your maximum. Of course, you can always manually make a larger offer if you really want the item.

When you win a bid, you and the seller get in touch with each other via e-mail. The seller will tell you the shipping charges, you then send them a check or money order, and they send you the item. There are also escrow services available. These charge a small fee to the buyer but allow them to pay by credit card. The funds are not released to the seller, who must agree to usethe escrow service, until the merchandise is received. See `http://www.iescrow.com` for more information on escrow services.

All in all, it is a great way to buy interesting items that you may not be able to find locally.

Pick Your Items Wisely

Before bidding on an item, make sure it is what you want to spend your money on and that the seller is reputable.

Read the description carefully, and if there is a picture, look at it closely. If you have any questions, send an e-mail to the seller. Most auctions give you the e-mail address of the seller along with the item. If it is not listed, you can get it easily. With eBay, for example, every item shows the seller's eBay registration name. Sometimes the name is their e-mail address, so all you need to do is just click it to send them an e-mail. Other times, you'll need to click their eBay name and enter your own eBay name and password to obtain the seller's e-mail. If the seller does not respond to you at all, think twice about making a bid.

Look for similar items by other sellers. Auctions let you search by keyword or by category. With millions of items for sale, it may take some time, but you'll get a clearer picture of an item's worth.

In fact, included on the CD with this book is the program eBay Crawler. While you are in eBay's own search facilities, you can open eBay Crawler on your screen. The eBay Crawler screen is shown here:

To search using eBay Crawler, enter a keyword for the item; select the way the list is sorted, the auction type, and what you want to search; then click GO. The program will connect to eBay by launching your Web browser if it is not already online; it will then display the search results in the eBay window.

NOTE Search for completed auctions to see what items actually sold for. This gives you a better gauge of value than the asking price.

Check the feedback rating of the seller. The feedback rating is the way the auction site keeps everyone honest. After completing a transaction, the buyer and seller can leave a comment about each other—either positive or negative.

In the screen that describes the item for auction, you will see a number following the seller's name. This number represents the feedback rating, which is roughly the number of positive comments minus the number of negative comments. A large feedback number indicates that the seller is active and has completed a number of transactions successfully.

Click the feedback number to read all of the comments, looking for negative remarks from unhappy buyers. Just bear in mind that it is impossible to please everyone all of the time, and some folks just can't be pleased at all.

Winning Strategies

When you find an item you want to bid on, don't jump into it with your maximum bid. Use some of these techniques to help get the item at the right price.

Check the date and time the bidding for the item ends. It will be shown along with the auction listing. If you will be available at that time, you'll be able to get online and follow the bidding, so you can make a last minute high bid before anyone else can outbid you.

Don't be the first to bid on an item. There are some folks who just love the competition. They may not bid on an item if they don't think anyone else is interested in it. So wait until the last possible moment to show any interest with your first bid, or with raising a previous bid on the item. If you wait until the end, you might get in when everyone else is offline.

Don't be the only bidder on an item. If you see the item going off auction without a bid, don't be the only bidder. Wait until the auction is done, then contact the seller by e-mail and ask if they are still interested in selling it. You may be able to purchase the item for the minimum bid, or even less, directly from the seller.

If you do not get the winning bid, send a note to the seller asking if they have any additional or similar items. They just might, and you can negotiate with the seller yourself.

47 Hard to Find Collectibles

EBay and other online auction houses aren't the only places to locate antiques and collectibles. There are plenty of online sources, both commercial and private.

It's All in the Search

Locating items is really an exercise in searching the Internet. It can be time-consuming, but it is usually well worth the effort. As your search abilities improve, you'll be able to locate items more quickly, and you'll build up a Favorites or Bookmarks list.

Here's What You Need

You'll need access to the Internet and some time to search in order to use the tips provided here. Using the program Collectibles ieBook, which you'll find on the CD with this book, will help you get started.

Sites and Features

When you're searching for a hard-to-find item, use all of the techniques that you learned about in Section 5, *Supercharge Your Searches.* Unfortunately, even the best search techniques can result in thousands of items being listed, especially if you use multiple search engines.

Collectibles ieBook

The best place to start is by using the program Collectibles ieBook. You'll find a copy of the program on the CD with this book.

Running the program displays the Table of Contents window, which appears as a series of notebook pages listing online sources of antiques and collectables, as shown in Figure 47.1. Each listing shows the source's name, category, and subcategory of items in which each specializes.

Browse through the book using the PgDn and PgUp buttons to locate a listing that interests you, and then click the listing to open its Details window, as shown in Figure 47.2. To go to the site to search for collectables, start your Web browser and then click the Get button in the Collectibles ieBook window.

While the program comes with a number of interesting sources, you can add your own as you find them. Click the New button at the bottom of the program window to open a blank details page. Enter the information about the site, selecting from the Category and Subcategory lists.

NOTE Before purchasing an item online, look up the prices of similar items on eBay and other auctions to judge its value.

FIGURE 47.1 Collectibles ieBook table of contents

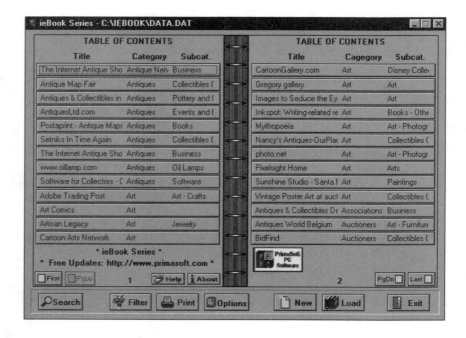

FIGURE 47.2 Details of an ieBook listing

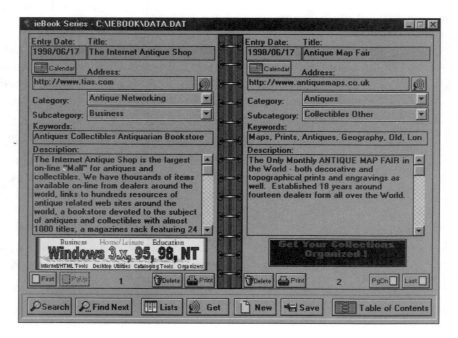

48 Online Investing

While the market has its ups and downs, there's money to be made in stocks and mutual funds. Certainly there's some risk involved, but the rewards can be substantial. Use your computer and the Internet to buy and sell stocks, and to track your investments.

Buying and Selling Online

The Internet has put a lot of pressure on the traditional stockbroker. Trading through the Internet is fast and easy, and much less expensive than using a traditional broker. On the Internet, you can buy and sell stocks for as little as $5.00 per trade. Try getting that from your broker!

Here's What You Need

You'll need access to the Internet, and you'll need to register with an online brokerage. You may have to provide a credit card number, send a check as a deposit for your trades, or establish credit through your bank or current broker, if you have one. On the CD with this book, you'll find two programs that help you track your investments once you get set up.

Sites and Features

If you are just looking for stock quotes—before you place an order or just to check your portfolio—look on the home pages of most ISPs. Usually they offer an investing link, and this is a good place to start. Many ISPs, such as AOL, CompuServe, and AT&T WorldNet, let you maintain a database of your stocks for instant tracking. When you log onto the investing area, you'll see the updated values of your stocks. At AT&T WorldNet, for example, your portfolio is maintained free by the Thomson Investors Network, which offers these features:

◆ Real Time Quotes

◆ Portfolio Tracker/Flash Mail

◆ First Call Center

◆ Stock Center

- ◆ Mutual Fund Center
- ◆ Investor Education Center
- ◆ Help

All of the major search engines have links to investing information. Over at Yahoo!, click the Stock Quotes link to search for a quote using this form:

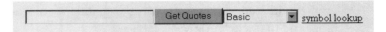

NOTE You can go directly to the Yahoo! stock quotes site at `http://finance.yahoo.com`.

Enter the symbol for the stock in the first text box, and choose the extent of information you want in the drop-down list. The options are Basic, DayWatch, Fundamentals, Detailed, Chart, and Research. Then click Get Quotes.

If you don't know the symbol, click *symbol lookup* or go to `http://finance.yahoo.com/l`. In the box that appears, enter the name of the company and click Lookup. You can also click Alphabetical Listing for a list of companies.

From the Excite.com home page, click stock quotes. Enter the symbol, select the information you want, and then click Go. Click *Symbol Lookup* to find the stock's symbol.

At Lycos, go directly to its stock quotes and information page at `http://investing.lycos.com`.

Most of the major stock brokerages have their own sites for getting account information and placing buy or sell orders. You can get the lowest commissions, however, from firms that specialize in online trading. At Brown and Company (`http://www.brownco.com`), you can purchase stocks for as little as $5.00 per trade, and options as low as $10.00 per trade.

To place orders at deep discounts on commission, try these sites:

`http://www.abwatley.com`	A. B. Watley, Inc.
`http://www.accutrade.com`	Accutrade

`http://www.ameritrade.com`	Ameritrade
`http://www.brownco.com`	Brown and Company
`http://www.etrade.com`	E*trade
`http://www.netinvestor.com`	The Net Investor
`http://www.tradeoptions.com`	TradeOptions
`http://www.vanguard.com`	Vanguard

If you are concerned about the dependability of online trading, check out `http://www.sonic.net/donaldj`. At this site, you'll find ratings for online discount brokers based on customer feedback. The ratings are updated twice a month.

There are a lot of other investing and financial sites on the Internet. For investment advice, for example, check out The Motley Fool (`http://www.fool.com`). You can apply to get a free credit report online from `http://www.consumerinfo.com`. You should also check with your bank for online banking information. Many banks let you transfer funds and pay bills over the Internet or by using programs such as Microsoft Money, Managing Your Money, and Quicken.

Getting Help

While a lot of the information on the Internet is interesting and fun, much of it can be downright helpful. When you have a question about almost anything, you can usually find an answer—or a place to go for an answer. You can always just type a keyword or two in any search engine and go from there. For some hints on how to find help on some specific matters, read on!

49 Driving Lessons— Making the Most of Your Drivers

Windows is driven by software drivers. To get your modem, monitor, mouse, and other peripherals working together as a computer, Windows needs special files, called *drivers*, for each peripheral. Some of the drivers are built right in to Windows, and some come with the disk packaged with the peripheral.

Get the Latest Drivers

If you are having problems with part of your computer, you may not have the latest drivers installed. Over time, the companies that make computer hardware improve and refine their drivers for optimum performance. There may be updated Windows 98 drivers specifically designed for a piece of hardware made before Windows 98 came about. Using the Internet, you can get the latest drivers, as well as news about your hardware, to keep that computer of yours humming.

Here's What You Need

All you will need is access to the Internet, and enough disk space to store downloaded drivers.

Sites and Features

The first place to look for the most recent drivers is on the home page of the company that made your hardware. Most manufacturers provide a library of drivers for all of their hardware, along with installation instructions and other information. Also look for a section on frequently asked questions (FAQ) to learn from the experiences of others.

If you have a Zoom modem, for example, go to `http://www.zoom.com` and look for modem drivers. You can usually find the company's Web site address in the manual packaged with the software. If not, try `http://www.companyname.com` (substituting in the name of the company, of course), or do a search for the company's name in any search engine.

If you have Windows 98 and Microsoft Internet Explorer 5 or later, you can check for updated drivers and other Windows files automatically by following these steps:

1. Select Windows Update from the Start menu. Windows dials into your Internet provider and begins a process of checking for newer files and recommended additions. Go directly to the site at any time at `http://windowsupdate.microsoft.com`.

2. When the site opens click the link *Product Updates*. You'll be asked to wait as it customizes the update process for your computer, and then you'll see programs in these categories of updates:

  ◆ Critical Updates

  ◆ Picks of the Month

  ◆ Recommended Updates

  ◆ Additional Windows Features

  ◆ Fun and Games

  ◆ Device Drivers

3. Click the check boxes for the items you want to update and then click Download.

Microsoft may not have all of the device drivers for your hardware. Rather than go to each manufacturer's site, you can try several sites that specialize in links to the latest drivers from the major, and some minor, players in the Windows hardware field.

Windrivers (`http://www.windrivers.com`), for example, has direct links to the driver sites of hundreds of manufacturers. You can also search for drivers. By clicking Advanced Search on the Windrivers home page, you can search by company name or the device category, as shown in Figure 49.1.

FIGURE 49.1 Finding device drivers at windrivers.com

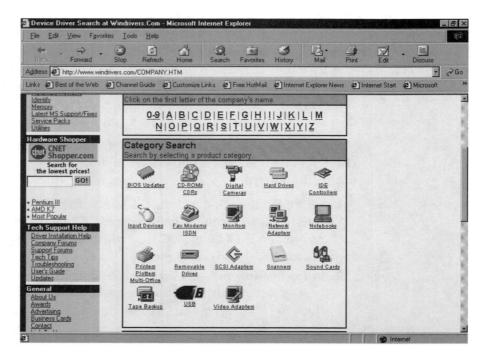

You can also locate generic drivers, run-time files, boot disks, and other common files. You can find drivers by the device's Federal Communications Commission (FCC) ID number, which is stamped on almost all pieces of computer equipment.

NOTE If you're still having trouble finding your driver, click Beginner Search in the Windrivers home page for detailed information.

Another excellent source for drivers is Drivers Headquarters (http://www.drivershq.com). On the first screen that appears, click the graphic of the wizard for a list of the categories of drivers shown in Figure 49.2. Click a link to access a listing of manufacturers, from which you can locate the drivers you need.

FIGURE 49.2 Drivers at Driver Headquarters

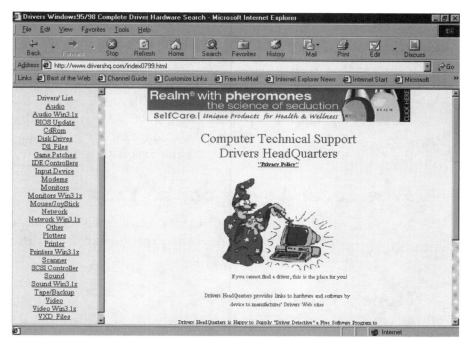

NOTE If you still can't find your driver, you can sign up for a free membership in DriverGuide.com (http://www.driverguide.com), which takes you step-by-step through locating and installing the driver you need.

If you want to look for updates to programs as well as drivers, you can try the program Catch-UP that is included on the CD with this book. Installing the program associates the Catch-UP Scanner as a helper application to your browser. To upgrade your software, go to the site http://www.manageable.com/execute.html and click the Catch-UP Now! button. The Catch-UP Scanner identifies your software programs and drivers, and then searches the Internet for upgrades.

50 I'm Going to Call My Lawyer! But before I Do...

The law is a very complex thing, with various interpretations depending on the state where you live. When you need a lawyer, nothing beats finding one in your area, sitting down, and explaining the issues. But a good place to start fighting your legal battles is on the Internet.

Free Legal Advice on the Web

While you can't go to court via the Internet—yet—you can find a lawyer when you need one. You can also get legal advice to help you through some troubled times.

Here's What You Need

All you will need is access to the Internet.

Sites and Features

As usual, there are hundred of places on the Internet to get legal information and advice. Most of the major law schools have Web sites, as do many legal firms.

Most of the sites include articles about various legal issues, links to legal sites, and often links to specific lawyers or a search engine to locate a lawyer near you.

The place I like to start for legal help, however, is DMS-Lawyer (http://www.dms-lawyer.com), sponsored by the firm of Dessen, Moses & Sheinoff in Philadelphia, PA shown in Figure 50.1. At this site, you can send an e-mail to a real live lawyer and get a personal response in return (usually from one of the firm's partners, not just a legal assistant).

When you get to the site, click the *Ask Us a Question* link at the bottom of the page. This will launch your e-mail program so you can send DMS-Lawyer your question.

FIGURE 50.1   Online legal help from dms-lawyer.com

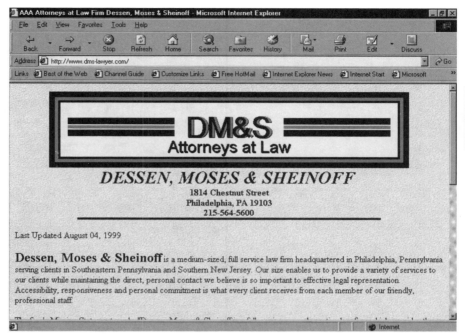

There are other links on this site that will let you access a library of legal resources, and access the Legal Article Wall where you'll find articles on current legal issues.

Another place to try for legal information is `http://www.freeadvice.com`. As you can see in Figure 50.2, this site has links to legal information of all sorts and a legal directory to help you find an attorney in your area.

A similar site, `http://www.lawyers.com`, lets you find an attorney based on practice area and location. There are also links to all sorts of information, message boards, and chat rooms where you can get personal advice.

Now as I said, there are hundred of places on the Internet to get legal information and advice. Here are a few other sites that provide generalized legal help and links to additional sites:

- ◆ `http://www.legal-link.com`
- ◆ `http://www.legalaccess.com.au/start.html`
- ◆ `http://db.legal.net/ldn/welcome/query.cfm`
- ◆ `http://www.alllaw.com`

FIGURE 50.2 Freeadvice legal help

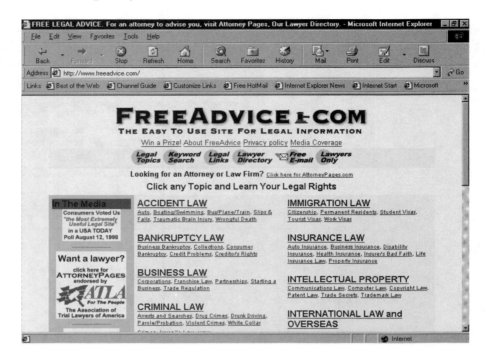

Some other interesting specialty sites include

`http://www.uni-sol.com/cca/index3.html`   Provides help repairing damaged credit.

`http://www.legalpadjr.com`   Specializies in legal advise for youngsters.

`http://www.divorcesupport.com`   Helps with a divorce or other marital problems.

`http://uscode.house.gov`   Provides access to general and permanent laws of the United States.

Most of the legal support sites on the Internet are sponsored by legal firms or other organizations. Although altruistic in their offer of information and advice, their ultimate goal is to obtain clients. This does not diminish the usefulness or accuracy of the information they provide, but you should proceed with caution.

51 Finding Health and Medical Advice Online

If you have a medical emergency, don't start looking for information on the Internet. But for background and reference information, and details about the medications you're taking, the Web is the perfect place to explore.

Is There a Doctor in the House?

While the computer is no substitute for a good doctor, it contains a wealth of useful information that can help you in many ways. Information that you can obtain on specific medications, for example, can prevent drug interaction and overdose accidents.

Here's What You Need

You'll need access to the Internet. For information about a medication, you'll need the name of the drug, its category of medication, and/or a sample of the medication to help identify it.

Sites and Features

Links for health and medical information are all over the Internet. You'll find them on ISP home pages and on all of the major search engines. For example, you can check out these search engine sites for information on specific conditions:

- ◆ http://dir.lycos.com/Health/Conditions_and_Diseases
- ◆ http://dir.yahoo.com/health/diseases_and_conditions

You can also look for the home pages of hospitals and medical centers, pharmaceutical companies, drug store chains, and medical equipment manufacturers.

For current information on medications, medical tests, and procedures, consider consulting Laurus Health at http://www.laurushealth.com.

If you want to research current literature for medical information, try Internet Grateful Med (`http://igm.nlm.nih.gov/`). This site, sponsored by the National Institute of Health, offers research through these medical databases:

Aidsline	Airsdrugs	Aidstrials	Bioethicsline	ChemID
DIRLINE	HealthSTAR	HSRPROJ	Medlne	Oldmedline
Popline	Spaceline	Toxline		

For information about your child's health, try these sites:

Your Kids Health (`http://www.yourkidshealth.com`)   Specializes in pediatric information, including how to reduce Sudden Infant Death Syndrome (SIDS).

Dr. Paula (`http://www.drpaula.com`)   Answers questions about your baby's health.

RxList and the Drug Information Database

For detailed information about medications, two great places to start are RxList (`http://www.rxlist.com`) and the Drug Information Database at Stayhealthy.com (`http://www.infodrug.com`).

At RxList, shown in Figure 51.1, you can search for drug information by the drug's name, keywords, and by the ID number imprinted on most capsules and pills. You can also see a list of the top 200 drugs prescribed in the last four years.

Once you locate the medication, you can get detailed information from one of these categories:

Description   Explains the category of the medication, what the drug consists of, and other general information about it.

Clinical Pharmacology   Explains how the medication works.

Indications, Dosage, and Administration   Details the conditions the medication is used to treat, the dosages it is available in, and how the medication should be taken.

Warnings, Contraindications, and Precautions   Explains who should not take the medication.

Adverse Reactions and Drug Interactions   Summarizes reported side effects of the medication and documented interactions with other medications.

Overdosage   Details how to respond to an overdose.

Patient Information   Gives general information that the user should be aware of.

FIGURE 51.1   **Get medication information at RxList**

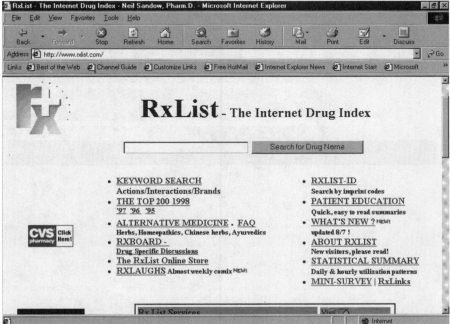

The Drug Information Database, supplied by Stayhealthy.com, has similar options and information. You can search for the medication by entering its name or starting with an alphabetical list.

To search by name, type the drug's name, or the beginning characters of its name, in the text box that appears in the Infodrug.com home page. Then click Find Now to see a list of drugs. Click the one that you want information about. A typical medication page is shown in Figure 51.2. Categories of information include the following:

◆ Common Uses

◆ How to Use

◆ Cautions

◆ Possible Side Effects

◆ Before Using

◆ Overdose

◆ Additional Information

FIGURE 51.2 **Sample of the Drug Information Database**

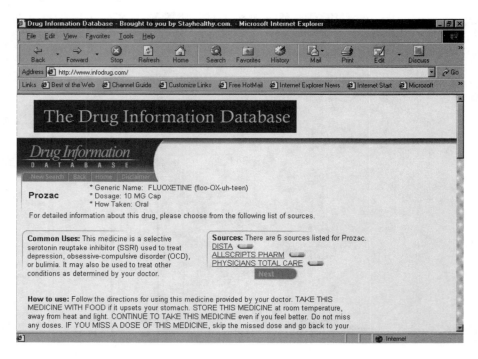

The icon of a capsule next to one of the sources listed indicates that a detailed photograph of the medication is available by clicking the source.

You can also search for a drug by using an alphabetic index. You'll see buttons labeled A through Z on the Infodrug.com home page. Click the button for the letter that starts your medication to see several ranges of names, such as P–Panc, Pand–PE-C, and so on. Click the range in which your medication is listed. In the list of links that appears, click your medication to read its detailed description.

InfoDrug, by the way, is operated by the same company that offers Stayhealthy.com (http://www.stayhealthy.com), an excellent portal to health and fitness information of all types.

Now don't bet your life on the health and medical information you can get over the Internet. While most of it is accurate, much medical information needs to be interpreted by a physician in light of your symptoms. What you can get over the Internet is information to make you a wiser health consumer. This information may also fill in some answers that you did not get from your physician. Message boards and online support groups are wonderful resources for information, supportive words, and help in locating the proper medical care.

52 Fixing Things at Home

Whether you are an experienced do-it-yourselfer or trying your hand at home repair for the first time, fixing something yourself can be a rewarding and money-saving experience. But as with most things in life, it pays to be prepared.

Prepare and Then Do

Before tackling that home improvement job, make sure you have the correct tools and parts you need, and you know how to do it. You can get all of this information over the Internet (except for the tools, of course). And, if you find out you don't feel like doing it yourself, you can find someone to do it for you.

Here's What You Need

The only thing you will need is an Internet connection.

Sites and Features

If you need some information about a specific product or tool, try the manufacturer. Some places to start are

`http://www.andersenwindows.com` Provides dimensions and information about doors and windows from Andersen.

`http://www.blackanddecker.com` Supplies information about using and selecting tools from Black & Decker.

`http://www.dremel.com` Allows access to the company catalog, parts pricing, and direction for ordering Dremel tools and accessories.

http://www.sears.com/craftsman Houses a catalog of Craftsman tools.

http://www.stanleyworks.com Provides information about tools, doors, hardware, and other products from Stanley.

Over at http://www.doityourself.com, shown in Figure 52.1, you can get information on projects of all sorts; you can also access bulletin boards to ask and answer questions about various subjects.

FIGURE 52.1 Look for how-to information at Doityourself.com

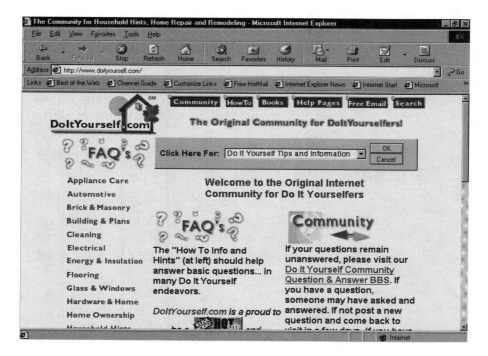

For links to manufacturers, builders, and other sources of information, try these links as well:

◆ http://www.build.com

◆ http://www.ehomeplans.com

◆ http://www.buildingonline.com

◆ http://www.buildnet.com

◆ http://www.buildernews.com

◆ http://www.buildtalk.com

AOL is the online arena of choice for a plethora of people, and it's obvious why. It's easy to use, it can be made safe for the youth of today, and yet there are nooks and crannies, tricks and secrets, that keep it interesting for the adventurers among us.

These numbered sections delve into the mysteries of AOL and beyond, from the banalities of cold cash to the fantastical programs you can use to augment your online experience. The only assumptions I'm making right off the bat are that you have AOL 4 and that you're somewhat comfortable with it. Otherwise, I let you in on all you need to know. From here on out, you're in AOL Land unless I say otherwise. Read on, and, above all, explore!

N O T E For more AOL tips and tricks, check out *America Online Amazing Secrets,* by Laura Arendal (Sybex, 1998).

53 Save Big Bucks

You have five different price options when you sign up for AOL.

Unlimited monthly   What it sounds like.

One-year plan   Unlimited access for one year, entirely prepaid, at what works out to be a slightly reduced monthly rate.

Limited plan   You pay a little bit less than half the regular monthly charge for a few free hours online per month. If you stay online past those few free hours (cumulatively, not per session), you will be charged a per-hour fee.

Light usage   The same idea as the limited plan, just *more* limited—and less expensive.

Bring your own access   Fondly referred to as BYOA, this plan allows you to use any other Internet Service Provider (ISP) to access the wonderful world of AOL; thus you pay slightly less than half of AOL's usual monthly fee, and if your ISP also charges less than the other half of AOL's monthly fee, you have unlimited access for cheap. Relatively, anyway.

Because you stand to save the most with BYOA, and because it's just slightly more obscure than the other options (being that you have to go outside the safe confines of AOL), I'll devote my discussion to this option.

NOTE All of these plans still won't protect you from being charged for hanging out in AOL's premium areas, like the supercool premium games offered through keyword **games**.

If you are unsure which plan will work best for you, check out your detailed bill at Help ➤ Accounts and Billing. In the AOL Billing Center window, click Display Your Detailed Bill (at bottom left). Choose Last Months Bill from the Request Detailed Billing Information dialog box. You will be treated to a list of the times any of your screen names accessed AOL during the previous billing period. The minutes you spent on AOL per session are listed in the Paid column. Add them up and divide by 60 (minutes/hour); did you spend more hours online than allowed under the light usage or limited access plans? If so—and if you're determined to spend less than the unlimited plan charges—BYOA might be for you.

NOTE If you decide you're going to go for one of the limited-access options, use Automatic AOL (found under the Mail Center menu) to keep your online hours low.

Bring Your Own Access!

The BYOA plan can be especially useful if you already have an account through school or work and wish to add AOL access on top of that; under these scenarios you will usually just be paying the BYOA fee. Plus you won't have to deal with modem traffic, as your school or work will most likely use a network connection to the Internet. This connection will be more direct—and possibly faster.

If you choose BYOA, some caveats are in order: you must always connect to the Internet through your ISP *before* signing onto AOL; otherwise you will be charged extra per hour of use. In addition, if your ISP is slow or overloaded, you may find your online experience a frustrating one. That said, many people are pleased as punch with BYOA.

WARNING If you want to access AOL through your work account, you'd best discuss it with your Systems Administrator first; some companies' firewalls need to be modified to allow AOL access from within, and some companies may just plain prohibit such a move.

Here's What You Need

First you need your own way to get on the Internet. Either an ISP—or a network that already has a way to connect to the Internet (such as you would find at work or school)—will do. If you don't have either, check out `http://www.thelist.com` for a comprehensive list of existing ISPs.

NOTE Each ISP is different; follow instructions provided by the ISP staff for installing the software and signing up.

You'll also need AOL software and a membership. Go to `http://www.aol.com` if you still need to sign up.

Here's How It Works

First you'll need to prepare your computer, and then you'll need to inform AOL's Billing department. Just follow me!

BYOA-ize Your Computer Setup

1. Open AOL (but don't sign on).

2. At the bottom of the Sign On window, click Setup.

3. Choose Create a Location for Use with New Access Phone Numbers or an ISP and click the Next arrow.

4. First glide down to the bottom of the dialog box and click the radio button next to Add a Custom Connection. Then, if you don't like the obvious but unexciting name AOL gives this connection, you can go for something more friendly, like *Myrtle*. Finally, click Next.

5. AOL will confirm that you are set up to use an ISP or LAN to connect. Click OK.

Notice, in the Select Location field at the bottom of your Sign On window, that your new connection, Myrtle, is showing. You still have the option to connect from the Home connection (incurring the extra charges associated with using AOL's access numbers) if you want or need to.

N O T E If your ISP or LAN is down and you *really* want to get online, you can minimize your cost by running an Automatic AOL session using an AOL access number to grab your mail. You'll only be charged for the scant minutes you're online fetching your mail, not for a full hour. Just remember to choose Home in the Select Location box before signing on.

Now connect to the Internet via your ISP or network. After you have established this connection, go back to AOL's Sign On window and make sure your new ISP/LAN connection (Myrtle) is showing in the Select Location field. Enter your AOL password into the Enter Password field, and click Sign On.

WARNING If you hear the modem shrieking at this point, you're signing on through AOL, not through your ISP. Click Cancel and go back through Steps 1 through 5, above.

BYOA-ize Your Bill

Now you need to change your billing plan to the BYOA option.

NOTE Your new BYOA billing price will take effect on the date that begins your next billing period. This monthly billing date is based on the date you signed up for AOL in the first place. To figure out your date, go to Help ≻ Accounts and Billing. In the AOL Billing Center window that appears, click Display Billing Date and Price Plan Info (at the bottom left of the screen under the View Your Bill heading). Your next billing date is the first line in the informative table displayed in the Billing Terms Explanation dialog box. This will be the date your BYOA charges will begin—as long as you sign up for BYOA 3 days before that date (72 hours before 10 A.M. of that date, to be precise).

Ready to make the switch? Get back to the AOL Billing Center window (Help ≻ Accounts and Billing) and click Change Your Billing Method or Price Plan.

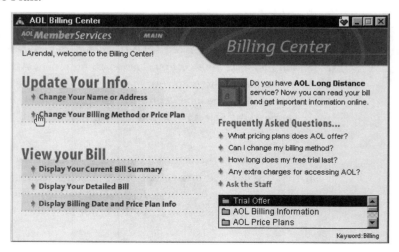

You'll be asked to enter your password, just to be on the safe side; do so and click Continue. Next choose Update Pricing Plan. In the resulting Change Price Plan dialog box, select Pending Plan. Under Price Plans, highlight BYOA, and then click the Select Plan button.

You're done! Don't spend your savings all in one place, now, y'hear?

54 Access AOL Anytime, Anywhere

Wouldn't it be great if e-mail were like phone mail? Pick up a phone anywhere in the world and you can dial into your voicemail and retrieve your messages. What if you could turn on a computer anywhere in the world and get your e-mail messages?

Well, now you can! NetMail is what makes it all possible. And it's yet another service available to you free—with your AOL membership.

Go Get 'Em with NetMail

With NetMail you can be anywhere in the world and receive and send your AOL mail from any computer that has Internet access. The interface looks almost exactly like your regular e-mail box, so really, you already know how to use it!

Here's What You Need

All you need is a computer that's hooked up to the Internet.

NOTE Of course, there could be compatibility issues—no program runs on every single platform ever invented—but NetMail is pretty easygoing. As long as the computer you're using runs at least Internet Explorer 3 or Netscape 3.02 and has Windows 3.1, 95, 98, or NT—or is a Mac—you're in business.

Here's How It Works

You're in Finland meeting your boyfriend's parents for the first time, you need a break from the whole family thing, and you desperately want to read your e-mail because your best friend promised she'd write you every day.

Just sneak up to his parents' den, turn on the computer, and connect to the Internet. Navigate to `http://www.aol.com` and click AOL NetMail. At the NetMail Sign-On screen, which looks like a small AOL Sign-On window, enter your screen name and password. Click Enter NetMail.

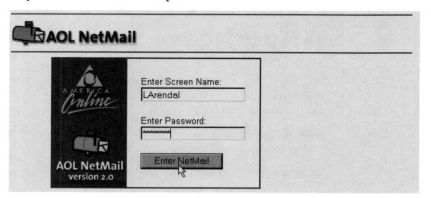

A dialog box informs you that the connection is secure; click OK. An interim sign-on screen assures you yet again that the connection you are about to make is secure, so don't flip when the usual "You are about to leave a secure Internet connection" dialog box appears. Click Please Click Here to Complete the Sign-In Process, wonder why AOL doesn't disable this "You are about to leave…" dialog box, then click OK.

You're in! You can see your new mail, old mail, and sent mail, write a letter, delete an e-mail, and, after you've read your e-mail, choose to keep it as new.

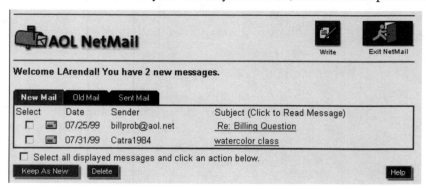

To read a message, just click once on the e-mail subject. From here you can move to the previous or following messages. After you are done reading, you could select any of the messages by clicking the check boxes in the Select column and either click Keep As New or Delete. Or you could just let the e-mail float to your Old Mail page.

The Old Mail and Sent Mail pages work just like they do in your AOL software; whatever time limit you've set for keeping old e-mails around will be honored by AOL NetMail.

You can send e-mail from here, too, but if you don't have an e-mail to reply to, you'd better have your friends' e-mail addresses memorized or written on your Send Postcards To list. You can't access your Address Book, stored cozily on your hard drive, from here.

To return to reality, just click Exit NetMail.

WARNING To keep your connection secure, AOL will boot you off Net-Mail if you dally in one place for more than 30 minutes, so don't plan on writing an e-mail novel this way.

55 Hey, AIM Buddy! Wake Up!

What, can you finally reach past the tenuous network connection between you and your AOL Instant Messenger (AIM) pals and, like a ringing phone, a buzzing doorbell, make them pay attention to you?

Yes, you can!

PowerAIM

Like any good add-on, PowerAIM (Powertools specifically for AOL Instant Messenger) adds more fun to your AIM frolic with the usual IM power-ups (spellcheck, multi-IM windows, etc.) as well as some features specially geared to getting those AIMs across.

Here's What You Need

You will need PowerAIM and AOL Instant Messenger. AOL Instant Messenger is available for free download from http://www.aol.com, and PowerAIM can be installed from the CD that accompanies this book.

Here's How It Works

Section 4 of *See It, Hear It, Say It* described the wonders of AOL Instant Messenger and its ability to connect you with any other AIMer anywhere on the Net. Now you can put a little pizzazz in that message with PowerAIM.

When you've installed it, launch PowerAIM. It will launch AIM with it—and expand the regular AIM window to accommodate the new features you are about to explore, as you can see in Figure 55.1.

FIGURE 55.1   **Bringing the instant message to a new level**

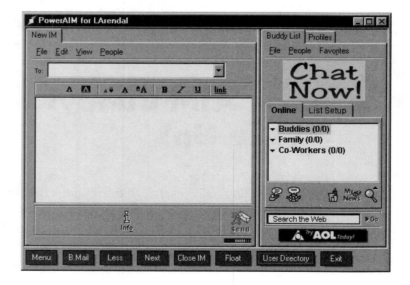

Not much has changed in the basic AIM window, though you do gain the ability to associate profiles and pictures with your AIM buddies in your AIM Buddy List.

The true power lies in the left window. Here you can do the regular PowerIM stuff; multiple windows, WAVs assigned to buddies, and so on.

Table 55.1 illustrates the differences between IM, AIM, PowerIM, and PowerAIM.

TABLE 55.1 You Say IM, I Say AIM...

Type of instant message	Description
IM (instant message)	You have IM capability with AOL, but only AOLies can send and receive IMs
AIM (AOL Instant Messenger message)	Available free from AOL's Web site, AIM allows AOLies and non-AOLies alike to send and receive instant messages
PowerIM	Take the plain ol' IM and add PowerTools, a BPS Software product
PowerAIM	Take your basic AIM and add PowerAIM, another BPS Software product

N O T E   For a more complete description of the capabilities of the PowerIM, see section 57.

Special to PowerAIM, though, is the ability to send and receive instant messages from your AIM buddies if they or you are offline. You can even opt for a WAV file to alert you when you have buddy mail waiting for you. To set these features up, read on.

First, you'll need to register with AIM's User Directory. To do so, click the User Directory button at the bottom of your PowerAIM window, then click Add Profile.

N O T E AOL users: do not be alarmed, I repeat, do not be alarmed, when you first try to get into the User Directory and Internet Explorer pops up and asks you to establish a connection to the Internet. Just follow the screens and tell it kindly that you already have a connection, thank you very much. The PowerAIM User Directory will continue to load in Internet Explorer, but will recognize your AOL connection from here on out.

In the Add to PowerAIM form that appears, enter your e-mail address, make up a password for the PowerAIM User Directory, and click Submit.

You can immediately access your new profile from the PowerAIM User Directory confirmation window, or you can edit it later. Or not—you really don't need to add a thing if you want to keep your PowerAIM matters private. But if you decide later on to add your name so long-lost friends can find you and send you Buddy Mail, click the User Directory button in your PowerAIM window, then click Edit Profile. After entering your AIM screen name and User Directory password, you'll be in.

Now for the fun stuff. To send a Buddy Mail, click the B.Mail button at the bottom of the PowerAIM window and choose Send a Buddy Mail Message. (Notice the other option is Read My Buddy Mail, which is where you'll go to retrieve your Buddy Mail when you get it.) Enter your AIM screen name and User Directory password. Once you're into the Leave a Message form, enter your buddy's screen name, your subject, and your message. When you're done, click Send.

N O T E Buddy Mail can be five lines long, max.

By default, PowerAIM will play a familiar-sounding "You have Buddy Mail!" WAV file when you receive Buddy Mail, whether you're online or off. You can associate a different WAV file with this occurrence—or turn the sound off—by going to the Menu button at the bottom of your PowerAIM window, clicking Options\Preferences, and fiddling with the options in the Buddy Mail corner of the PowerAIM Options window.

56 Nuisance-Free AOL?

Yes, Virginia, there is an ad-free, shriek-free, logoff-free AOL in your future! This section will tell you how to do all that and more.

No-Nuisance AOL

Of course, there are many annoyances—I mean, *features*—that can't be avoided. The AOL Today window's presence is one of them; trying to close it is especially annoying—because you can't. (I mean, really, why bother putting the Close button in the upper right corner if it's redundant with the minimize button?) But there are a surprising number of things you can do to rid yourself of pesky noises and people.

Here's What You Need

All you need for most of these quick fixes is your AOL connection and these instructions!

Here's How It Works

After reading the rest of this section, you should be able to get rid of Marketing ads, loud modems, annoying chatters and IMers, unwanted logoffs, and those Welcome and AOL Today windows that just won't quit.

Put an End to Ads

Take advertisements. Even US citizens, consumers that we are, enjoy an ad-free moment here and there. And we don't always want to know about the latest version of the automobile status symbol of the moment. Really, we don't.

Luckily, we can turn all advertising off in just a few fell swoops.

You'll have to be online to do this, so sign on now. Once you're on, go to My AOL ➤ Preferences. A dizzying array of options will swim before your eyes. Click Marketing, located on the bottom row.

Purple SweetTart-like buttons will tantalize you with the following options:

US Mail from other organizations (that AOL "occasionally" makes your name available to…)   You too can receive unwanted offers for items from software to apparel!

US Mail from AOL   Here you can be tempted to schill for AOL or buy AOL-sponsored material.

Telephone   Do you really want to get a call during dinner about the newest, hottest digital camera?

E-mail   All of the above, but through e-mail…

Pop-up   Same old, same old, appearing immediately after sign-on.

Additional information   This useful write-up tells you how to avoid marketing campaigns *nationwide* by registering with the Mail Preference Service and Telephone Preference Service.

NOTE   Only master screen names see pop-ups. So if you want to see these but don't want your progeny to, rest easy; AOL has taken care of it already.

To sign up for or, more likely, get rid of any of the above irritations, simply click the button next to the option you want to declare your preference on. A description of what you are about to prefer (one way or the other) appears; read it and click Continue. An even more detailed discussion about the ramifications of stating a preference can be scrolled through. Notice that your preferences will be respected for one year, after which time you will need to put your foot down again. After all, you could change your mind!

Click the radio button specifying which option you prefer (if you're reading this in eager anticipation, it will probably be the option beginning with *No*), and click OK.

After a few dialog boxes that inform you that your preference has been set—but if you change your mind don't forget to come on back—you're back at the Marketing Preferences window. Go right down the list until you're satisfied with your choices, then close the window and move on to eradicating another annoyance from your life!

....
N O T E Notice also that AOL reserves the right to send pop-ups, e-mails, and telephone calls your way if the information is deemed essential for you to have. Like I said, you can't fix all the, uh, features...

Kill Modem Sounds

Little did you know, you can make your modem louder! Maybe the neighbors in the apartments next door, above you, and below you all need to know when you're signing onto AOL.

Alternatively, you can make your modem softer—or just turn it off altogether.

If you're online, sign off. If you're on your computer but AOL isn't running, open it now (but don't sign on).

In the Sign On window, click Setup. Keep looking at the bottom of your screen; in the Setup window, click Expert Setup. In the Connection Setup dialog box, click the Devices tab to reveal the connection method(s) you've established. The modem you're using should have a check mark over its icon. Make sure it is highlighted (if it isn't, just click it) and click the Edit button in the lower-right corner. Speaker volume can be adjusted through the drop-down list in the lower-right corner of the Expert Edit Modem dialog box; click the drop-down arrow and choose your poison; off, soft, normal, or loud.

When you've made your choice, zoom over to the left side of the dialog box and click OK, then Close. You're home free!

Instant IM Rejection

There are three ways to deal with AOL members who bother you through IMs: report them, ignore them without actively shutting them out, or disallow IMs from them altogether.

To report the miscreant   When you receive an offensive IM, click the Notify AOL button at the bottom of your IM window immediately. Minimize any future IMs from the offender; the messages will stream in, but who can tell?

To ignore an irritant   If the IM isn't offensive and/or you don't feel like reporting the IMer, just minimize the IM window. Any other incoming IMs will appear in their own window(s) (one per screen name), and the inappropriate IM messages will continue to appear in your minimized IM window.

To block the bum   Go to My AOL ➤ Buddy List. In the Buddy List window, click the Privacy Preferences button.

Here you can allow all IMs, select a few you'll allow through, or block them all. Notice at the bottom of the window that you can block either just Buddy Lists or both Buddy Lists and IMs. Blocking Buddy Lists will prevent your name from showing up on another person's Buddy List when you sign on. Blocking IMs, well, that's what we're here for, right?

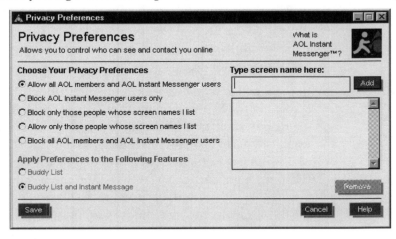

N O T E You can also block IMs from AOL Instant Messenger users through Buddy List Preferences. Even if you don't block an AIM user outright, you will always have the option to decline incoming AIM messages.

Enjoy the Chat Room

You don't have to put up with other chatters just because they're in your space; chat rooms really can be a good way to dialog about what you're interested in. Following are some hints to help you do just that.

Use a Special Screen Name If you're going to expose your screen name to the world of online wackos, some of which do reside on AOL, don't use your master screen name. Create a second—maybe more playful—screen name so you can lurk and meander wherever your curiosity takes you. This way you won't need to worry about future e-mails and IMs from weirdos while you're conducting serious business with your master screen name. Speaking of which, don't forget to turn off all e-mail and IMs to your chat screen name, unless you enjoy witless and sophomoric exchanges.

> **To create your chat screen name** Go to My AOL ≻ Screen Names. Click Create a Screen Name and follow the easy instructions.

> **To block IMs** See *Instant IM Rejection*, just above.

> **To block e-mail** Go to Mail Center ≻ Mail Controls. Click Set Up Mail Controls, choose the screen name you want to control, and click Edit. Here you can choose from a variety of settings such as: receive and send all e-mails, allow only select people to send you e-mail, block all e-mail, and so on. Notice that the Result box at the bottom of the window explains each option. When you have decided on your e-mail availability, click OK, then OK to the confirmation dialog box.

Ignore the Heck Out of 'Em Even with e-mail and IMs disabled, you'll still run into AOL members who are, shall we say, still finding their place in the world—and the chat rooms. Fortunately, you don't have to be part of their "self-exploration" (which, as I've said, tends toward the witless and sophomoric). If you're in a chat room and a chatter is becoming bothersome, you can shut them out with the Ignore feature. If you ignore them, you won't see their chatter on your screen (and if you've disabled e-mail and IMs to the screen name you're using, you have no worries about hearing from them).

WARNING Ignore only works as long as the Ignoree stays put. If they leave the chat room and then rejoin it, the Ignore spell you put on them will have lifted. Just Ignore them again.

To Ignore a chatter:

1. Notice to the right of the large chat box there is a list of the people currently enjoying the chat room. Double-click the screen name of the Ignoree-to-be.

2. In the Information About dialog box, click the check box next to Ignore Member.

Blissful silence ensues. Satisfying, isn't it?

57 Power It Up!

Want more bang for your AOL buck? More oomph per second than you'll know what to do with? Then this is the section for you. Herein are described enhancements you can make to AOL by installing PowerTools, an AOL-approved program that will astonish and delight you.

POWER IT UP! **259**

PowerTools

There are two versions of this magnificent program, both of which will transform your AOL look and feel and entire experience. PowerTools Pro is included on the accompanying CD. To get a copy of PowerTools Light, go to http://www.bpssoft.com.

PowerTools Pro   Is superuseful for power users who really want to soup up AOL, as well as for guides and hosts.

PowerTools Light Edition   Is easier on hard disk space and will go a bit more trippingly than PowerTools Pro.

Here's What You Need

Besides AOL, you need BPS Software's PowerTools. Install PowerTools Pro from the CD or download it from keyword **BPS**.

NOTE   BPS Software recommends that you have at least a Pentium 150 and 32MB RAM in order to run PowerTools Pro. It will function with less, but slowly. If you don't have quite this get-up-and-go in your computer, consider PowerTools Light.

Here's What You Can Do

There are two versions of PowerTools available: Pro and Light Edition. Pro gives it all to you, but Light can be easier on the first-time user. Read on to find out which one is for you.

PowerTools Pro

After you have installed PowerTools Pro from the CD, just double-click the PowerTools Pro icon on your desktop. It will launch and bring AOL with it.

Even before you sign on, your AOL window will be very different, as you can see in Figure 57.1!

FIGURE 57.1 Egad! I'm surrounded by PowerStuff!

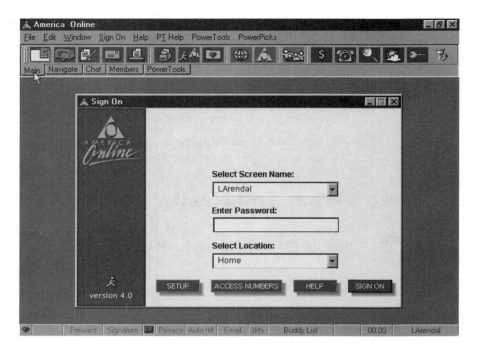

NOTE You can always launch AOL without PowerTools by double-clicking your AOL desktop icon.

Notice the toolbar tabs; each toolbar page allows you to do extra stuff with your regular AOL functions. The Main toolbar is pretty much as usual, but not entirely.

PowerTools main menu

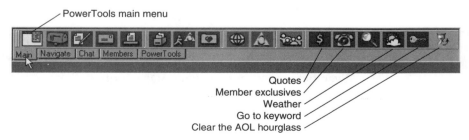

Quotes
Member exclusives
Weather
Go to keyword
Clear the AOL hourglass

PowerTools main menu Includes PowerTools Help, customization options, and Sign-Off (no prompt). Sign-Off (no prompt) allows you to sign off AOL without having to deal with the "Are you sure you want to sign off" dialog box.

Quotes, **Member Exclusives**, and **Weather** Do exist on the non-PowerTools AOL toolbar, but only if you've set your screen resolution to 1024×768.

Go to Keyword Gives you instant access to other keywords you've gone to as well as to the master keyword list found at keyword **keyword**.

Clear the AOL Hourglass Is another extra-special PowerPerq; if AOL ever stops you in your tracks with the busy hourglass, just click this button and it'll clear. Whatever you were doing will quit executing, too, but it's worth it.

NOTE You can change what your toolbar displays, so if you'd rather see the text descriptions for a button, you can add those (and you can choose where to add them!) or opt to replace the buttons with text. Simply right-click a blank spot on the toolbar and choose Toolbar Options. The "just buttons" option is the most compact—and colorful—so that's what you'll see in this chapter.

The Navigate toolbar is really no different from the regular AOL version, but it's prettier. The big enhancement, other than the addition of the PowerTools main menu, is the Keyword/Web Address field drop-down list. Click this drop-down arrow to see precisely the areas and Web pages you've gone to recently (including addresses from earlier online sessions!). You can then navigate back to these places without having to search your memory for the path you took to get there.

Enhanced keyword/Web address field

The Chat toolbar is entirely fresh.

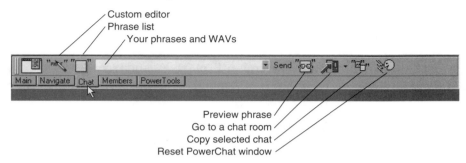

Custom editor
Phrase list
Your phrases and WAVs

Preview phrase
Go to a chat room
Copy selected chat
Reset PowerChat window

Custom Editor   Lets you organize, edit, and add to those phrases in your phrase list. PowerTools supplies its own phrases—from an ad for PowerTools, to the stock chat phrases we've all seen before, to quotable quotes.

Phrase List   Shows you your list of phrases.

Your Phrases and WAVs   Gives you a quick way to pick a phrase (like, *be back shortly*) and send it before bolting from your computer to the refrigerator and back.

Preview Phrase   Shows you exactly what the phrase you've selected in the Your Phrases and WAVs field looks like and gives you some tools for modifying it.

Go to a Chat Room   Click the drop-down arrow and select Create Your Own Chat to do just that. Realize the true power of this button by finding a chat room through People Connection (on the Main toolbar) that is completely full. When AOL helpfully informs you that the room is full and offers to take you to a less-crowded alternative, just click the Go to a Chat Room button on the Chat toolbar. PowerTools will bombard this room with attempts to get in until someone leaves, and voilà! You're in!

Copy Selected Chat   Copies the chat you've highlighted; you can then alter it and add it to your list of phrases, send it to someone, or save it for posterity.

Reset PowerChat Window   Reconnects PowerTools to your chat window in case it disconnects.

Your chat window will look different, too; check out Figure 58.2. Most of the new features are handy and self-explanatory. The Option button gives you all sorts of fancy options; you could spend days perfecting your welcome phrase, fonts, and colors; picking Hot Words so you can play the PeeWee Herman Word of the Day game (you know, when someone says the Word, everyone screams); programming your bursts… The Options drop-down arrow gives you even more versatility, including the ability to switch back to plain ol' AOL chat. The Effects button, which brings up the Effects toolbar you see at the bottom of Figure 57.2, allows you to colorize your pithy sentences.

FIGURE 57.2   Chattin' in style

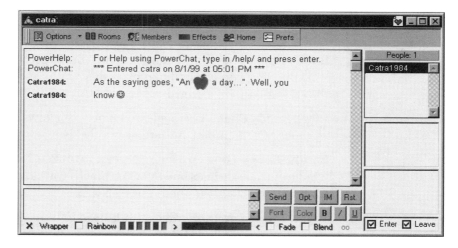

The Members toolbar encourages all sorts of interactive activities.

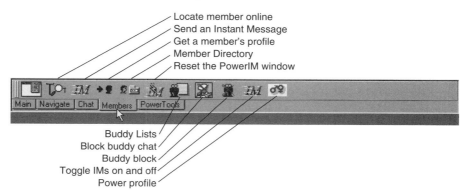

Locate Member Online   Is a power-enhanced version of the usual Locate Member feature; you can locate someone, send them an IM, add them to your Buddy List—all from here.

Send an Instant Message Brings up the Send IM window, with some extra options like immediate access to your canned phrases.

NOTE Section 55 takes the PowerIM further—into Internet territory, in fact.

Get a Member's Profile and **Member Directory** Are standard.

Reset the PowerIM Window Reconnects you to PowerTools if you become underpowered.

Buddy Lists Is also fairly standard, but you do get to have some fun with your buddies; you can assign nicknames, WAVs, and colors to them so they'll stand out in a crowd.

Block Buddy Chat Is a toggle that blocks or allows chat invitations sent by other AOL members from their Buddy Lists.

Buddy Block Pops up a colorful version of your Privacy Preferences window for Buddy Lists and IMs. The blocks you can set are the usual, but it's sure useful to get to them this easily.

Toggle IMs On and Off Click this button to have PowerTools send the *IM off* or *IM on* code to IM central.

Power Profile Connects you to BPS Software and lets you in on a little add-on that will manage the profiles you collect during your wandering chats.

When you receive an Instant Message, you'll notice immediately that the IM window is powered up now, too, as illustrated in Figure 57.3. If you had more than one incoming IM, each IM window would become accessible via a system of tabs.

Probably the Number One Cool Thing about PowerIMs is that you can type your message and just press Enter on your keyboard to send it. No more clicking Send, no more struggling to remember that the keyboard shortcut is Ctrl+Enter… just Enter. Like any other normal program.

FIGURE 57.3 **Catra amuses herself by self-PowerIMing.**

The PowerTools toolbar is the grooviest.

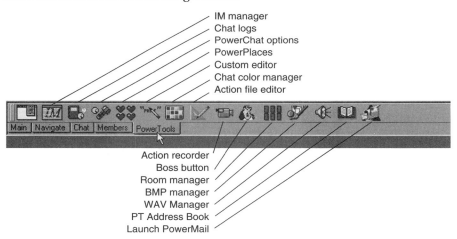

IM Manager Allows you to customize your IMs. Besides the usual handy extras like spellchecking, fonts'n'colors, and auto answering, IM Manager also makes it easy to autosave those IMs in logs. The best thing, though, is the priority password feature, which allows you to set a password that you then tell only Very Important AOL Members, who can use it to IM you even when you have IMs blocked.

Chat Logs   Shows you all the chats you've had. You can then transfer all those screen names to your address book or do things like log the time and room count every 15 minutes. I mean, who knew they needed to know that? Lucky for us, Chat Logs has corrected our ignorance.

PowerChat Options   Gets you to the chat options you can access from the Option button within a chat room window, which was described earlier in this section.

PowerPlaces   Is a souped-up Favorite Places, but it doesn't automatically load your faves into it. You can still access your pre-PowerTools favorites from the Main toolbar, but it is easier to just choose Tools ≻ Import AOL Favorite Places and access your old friends right here. With PowerPlaces you can group faves, place fave groups on the menu bar for instant access, and share faves with other AOLies via IM, chat, or e-mail.

Custom Editor   Is the same as on the Chat toolbar, discussed earlier in this section.

Chat Color Manager   Will make your chat and IM screens very colorful. You can assign fonts and colors to specific screen names, either permanently or for an online session only. This feature can really help a screen name stand out if, for instance, you're chatting with just one or two others in a crowded chat room.

Action File Editor   Lets you edit the actions you've recorded with the Action Recorder.

Action Recorder   Like Microsoft Word's macros, records your mouse movements and clicks so you can assign a shortcut key to an entire sequence of actions and have PowerAOL perform it for you. You can augment your sequence with the non-mouseable actions (such as Wait) found on the Action Recorder's Custom Actions list.

Boss button   First, open that spreadsheet you're working on, then open AOL on top of that. When your supervisor gets the urge to roam, just click the Boss and any trace of AOL will disappear from your screen and even from your taskbar. Your boss will never notice the inconspicuous gray and black icon over by your clock, but that's how you'll reactivate AOL after your supervisor has disappeared around the corner.

Room Manager   Shows you all the active chat rooms available to you, as well as those you've grouped in your Favorite rooms list, and gives you the option to go—or knock until you get in. One-stop chatting, right here.

BMP Manager   Tracks your BMP graphics files that are scattered all over your hard drive so you can access them quickly when you want to insert them into chats, e-mails, or IMs.

WAV Manager   Is like BMP Manager for WAV sound files. Especially cool is WAV Manager's AOL menu, which allows you to assign whatever sound you like to any of AOL's sound-triggering occurrences. "You've Got Mail" goes the way of the dinosaur!

PT Address Book   Imports and expertly manages all the addresses, photos, nicknames, and e-mails you want to save and group. It also exports your address files to another address book (for instance, in the next version of AOL) or to WordPad for use in other programs and for printing.

Launch PowerMail   Like Launch PowerProfiles on the Chat toolbar, lets you in on the power you can add to your mailbox for just a small add-on fee.

The PowerTools taskbar, sitting quietly at the bottom of your AOL window, adds some functionality and much one-click access.

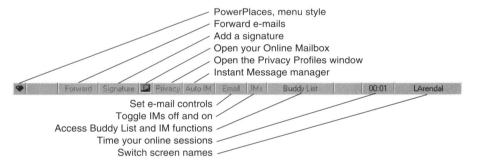

PowerPlaces   Grants you instant access to the areas and URLs you and PowerTools have added to your PowerPlaces.

Forward   Has three TOS addresses preset so you can effortlessly report harassing or junk e-mails to AOL's TOS folks. You can also add your own e-mail addresses to this list, like the group you often forward humorous e-mails to.

Signature   Adds a serious, funny, or custom-made signature to any e-mail, IM, or posting.

Open your Online Mailbox icon   Does what it says. No bells, no whistles.

Privacy   Opens the Privacy Profiles window discussed earlier in this chapter.

AutoIM   Opens the Instant Message Manager window, discussed earlier in this chapter.

Email   Allows you to quickly set who you allow or disable e-mail from.

IMs   Click once to toggle IMs off, and click once again to toggle IMs back on.

Buddy List   Accesses your Buddy List and sends IMs. This button will show your buddies' names in blue when they sign on, and in red when they've signed off.

Clock   Times your online sessions.

Screen Name   Remembers who you are, or, more likely, switches screen names.

Let me go on about just a few more great features, and then I'll let you go. In the menu bar, you'll notice you have a few more menu items. Go to PowerTools ➤ Misc ➤ AOL Window List. This window will list way more than the usual nine windows that fit on the AOL Window menu. Merely click the window you want to bring to the top, and it does your bidding.

Now go to your Windows taskbar and click the PowerTools taskbar button. Here you can, among other things, minimize the Upload Status window that appears when you're downloading software, games, attachments, whatever. After this window is minimized, you can do whatever you want. Your AOL session will be a bit slower during downloading, so you may want to stick with simple things like reading and responding to e-mail, but it's still a giant improvement over finding something else to do for 15 minutes.

Maybe the best thing about PowerTools is the most hidden. You can close the AOL Today and the Welcome windows simply by going to the AOL Windows menu and selecting these PowerTools-added items: Close the AOL Today Window and Hide/Show Welcome Window. Finally, the screens that will never die get their due!

Well, that just about sums up PowerTools Pro. Your turn to play!

PowerTools Light Edition

PowerTools Light Edition brings with it the following basic features. If these are enough for you, and/or if your computer won't run PowerTools Pro efficiently, PowerTools Light Edition is the power tool for you!

Buddy List   Lists nicknames, buddy group colors, special buddy WAVs.

Chat stuff   Organizes WAV files, WAV colors, WAV bursts, delayed WAV bursts, and canned phrases.

IMs   Contains priority passwords, one-window IM management, sending with Enter, and auto spellcheck.

Cool miscellanae   Includes signatures, hourglass cursor clearing, and upload status window minimizing.

You can download PowerTools Light Edition from keyword **BPS**.

PowerVault

A close relation to PowerAIM and PowerTools, the cleverly named Power-Vault will get you leaping about AOL and the Internet with ease, as well as cracking the whip on archiving and privacy.

With PowerVault, you can launch AOL and get onto any Web site (even those that require your login and password) with one command. In addition, you can back up and restore anything, as well as encrypt myriad AOL features, such as your Personal Filing Cabinet.

You can even remind yourself to change your password once every two weeks—and then not bother to remember your new one. Just remember your password to PowerVault, and it will take care of the rest.

Install PowerVault from the CD—or download it from keyword **BPS**.

INDEX

Note to the Reader: In this index **boldfaced** page numbers refer to primary discussions of the topic; *italics* page numbers refer to figures.

FREE SETUP
$25
Savings

Get

Rocket-Fast

Internet Access
With All the Perks!

- Unlimited Internet access at speeds up to 56k

- Local access nationwide and international roaming capabilities

- Free, reliable email

- Free 6MB of webspace for your own Web site

- A fully customizable Personal Start Page[SM]

- 24/7 toll-free customer service and tech support

- Free subscription to bLink™, Earthlink's member magazine

- Free software like QuickTime™, RealPlayer®, and Shockwave®

And much more!

Earthlink Sprint launches you into the Web with unlimited access at speeds up to 56k and more local access numbers than any other ISP.

www.earthlink.net

EarthLink
Sprint

Call Now!

1-800-Earthlink (327-8454)   **Mention Reg. #400037787**

What's on the CD

The CD packaged with this book contains over 50 programs that will make surfing the Internet faster, more interesting, and certainly more fun. Here's a sample of the programs you'll find—see the readme.txt file on the CD for a complete list of programs, installation instructions and descriptions. (On the CD these products are arranged in alphabetical order, but here they have been grouped by the section of the book in which they are discussed.)

Internet Tool Pack (discussed in the introduction) Contains some basic programs you'll need for your travels through the Internet.

  ClipCache   Lockdown 2000   NeoPlanet   WinZip

See It, Hear It, Say It Enjoy multimedia, make your own CD's, watch the world go by, and communicate with the world from the comfort of your own chair.

  EarthTuner   MP3 CD Maker   PowWow   RealPlayer

Searching the Unlimited Resource Get help finding all sorts of things over the Web.

  Copernic99MP3 FiendSearch By MediaSearch Master DemoShetty Search

It's About Time Track your online time, tell time, and be on time!

  CMDTime   EZE Clock   Gtime   Modem Logger
  Online Time   TimeIt!   Total Timer   WinAnalyzer
  World Clocks   WorldTime2   YATS32

News and Mail Stay informed about the latest news, don't miss an e-mail ever again, avoid Spam, and get free e-mail accounts.

  NewsWatch   PureMail   Ristra Mail Monitor   SpamEater Pro   Spam Off

More Free Stuff Get free offers from all around the Internet while they last!

  Barking Cards   Download Assistant   Earthlink   GetRight